# FIRST TIME IN PAPERBACK!

# THE CRADLE WILL FALL

## CARL S. BURAK, M.D., J.D., & MICHELE G. REMINGTON

*"The Cradle Will Fall* **is sad and captivating."**
—*Los Angeles Times*

*The Cradle Will Fall* is the extremely dramatic and heart-wrenching story of Miclele Remington, a loving wife who very much wanted to be a mother. Yet weeks after returning from the hospital, she killed her infant son, then turned the gun on herself—only to survive.

A unique collaboration between Michele and her psychiatrist, Carl S. Burak, M.D., J.D., *The Cradle Will Fall* is a riveting portrait of a woman suffering from postpartum depression. What might seem to many an unpardonable crime is revealed as a frightening yet foreseeable and treatable symptom in the life experience of millions of women.

"The story of Michele Remington will break your heart....*The Cradle Will Fall* is a story of triumph as a woman, a family, and a community learn to understand and forgive."—*Grand _____ Press.*

D1026283

# T H E
# CRADLE
# WILL
# FALL

## CARL S. BURAK, M.D., J.D., & MICHELE G. REMINGTON

**LEISURE BOOKS**    NEW YORK CITY

A LEISURE BOOK®

March 1996

Published by special arrangement with Donald I. Fine, Inc.

Dorchester Publishing Co., Inc.
276 Fifth Avenue
New York, NY 10001

DONAHUE® transcript courtesy of Multimedia Entertainment, Inc

For further information, contact: Donald I. Fine, Inc., 19 West 21st Street, New York, NY 10010

# Acknowledgments

During the six years we were working on *The Cradle Will Fall* I was very aware of my dual role as physician and co-author. I was prepared to abandon the book if it seemed to interfere with Michele's therapy, or if Michele for any reason simply did not wish to continue. Neither happened and I want both Michele and Jeff to know that I appreciate their determination, respect and courage in allowing the world to witness their anguish so that others might benefit.

Over these years of writing I've enjoyed the love, support, insight and enthusiasm of many people. I'm sure I've forgotten some, and for those I've remembered my words will often be inadequate.

My wife Ronnie is my partner, friend and the context of my happiness. My son Eli is the light of my life and his gift of love is immense. You both fill my heart with joy.

My father Samuel passed away in 1969. My mother Belle continues to live with vitality. I hope my father can hear me. I thank you both for your gift of life and so much more. I was so lucky.

To others in my family, Ed and Shirley Shils, Connie, Bob, Gary and Jay Rubinstein, Johanna Bates, Barry Shils, Nancy Shils, Max Szczurek and Serena Lyde. I love you all.

To Bill Falik, Diana Cohen, and their children Abby, Rebecca and Ben. Exceptional friends whose love and support I cherish.

To Barbara Zitwer and Lois de la Haba, literary agents whose passion and belief in this work will forever be appreciated.

To Donald Fine for not being afraid to publish a book in which the topic, first heard, sometimes evokes a gasp.

To Jason Poston for his help with editing and so many other things.

To Mark Keller and Norman Blais who were generous in sharing their legal documentation and their heart and soul in Michele's defense.

To Nancy Berchthold who having survived her own difficulty established the group "Depression After Delivery" which has been helpful to so many.

A thousand roses to Linda Lake, Dee and Glen Ertell, Marge Roberts, Nicki Forrest, and especially to Diane McPhail, all of whom supported with patience the physical process of creating and recreating and recreating and recreating the manuscript.

To Francey Green, the first to read the rough draft. When she told me with tears in her eyes that she read through the night in order to finish, I began to have hope.

To Bob and Helen Pezzulich for their special kindness.

To Fred Loy for his sensitivity, both professionally and simply as a human being.

This book would probably not have been written were it not for Ann Malamud and her husband Bernard, the Pulitzer Prize winning author. In 1980, whenRonnie, Eli and I moved from San Francisco to Bennington we bought a home next door to the Malamuds. They were warm, supportive, caring people. Bernard's writing is very psychologically attuned and I think he was always interested in his psychiatrist/psychologist neighbors.

I would often say to Bern, "I really want to write." He would reply "so write." In 1983, following open heart surgery Bernard Malamud suffered a stroke from which he slowly recovered. He demonstrated enormous determination and resilience in returning to his work.

On a cool, brilliant October day in 1984, the day before the Malamuds were to return to New York City for the winter, I went next door to say goodbye. Bernard was napping and Ann engaged me in a conversation during which I explained an idea I had for a book, (another of those imaginary enterprises about writing which so often occupied my fantasy). Ann became intrigued and when Bernard awakened she told him of the idea. He took notes (which I've since framed), and then proceeded to call his agent. The agent was interested in the idea and suggested that I send a synopsis.

The synopsis was horrible, but I had at least put pen to paper. I never stopped. My daily writing habit had persisted for four years by the time Michele asked for help. During those four years I learned a great deal. Although the book that Iinitially started was never near completion, the process made it possible to at least tackle the writing of *The Cradle Will Fall*. To Bernard Malamud, may he rest in peace, and to Ann Malamud, I extend my deepest appreciation.

Finally, to so many other friends and associates who have read, listened, suggested, tolerated, guided, and supported, Michal and Tom Alkoff, Dave Brown, Paul Dolmetsch, Aliceand Chuck Drayton, Hester Duffield, Judy and Saul Eisen, Rosemary and Jamie Fletcher, Jill and Jim Fuson, Rita Green, Lucy Hopkins, Shana Houlihan, Belle Huang and Ed Blumenstock, Roberta Huberman and Stu Schwartz, Carol and Bob Kafin, Ken Kensinger, DonKowalski, Jane Lewis, Lanie and Ron Mensh, Claire Merritt, Mary Mohit, Sally Mole and Dale Guldbrandsen, Gloria Moore, Shelly Olliff, Kristin and Lou Propp, Andi and Steve Risen, Theresa St. Helaire, Pat and Bruce Samuels, Elana Schrader-Coren and Michael Coren, Cathi and Ron Shapiro, Alexandra Simmonds, Sally Sise, Jan and Jeff Slavin, Sue and Tom Snyder, Anne and Doug Stewart, Marie and Bud Tachirhart, Randy Wainwright, Jan and Sandy Weimer, and Tracy Williams. I thank you all.

—CARL S. BURAK, M.D., J.D.

Most of you who are reading these words could not possibly understand how I feel. Despite that, my need to share what happened has grown stronger with each passing day. It is my hope that someone, somewhere, might be helped because of my openness.

As I began to write, the first pages about my childhood and young adult years came relatively easily. I was even able to describe the time that I learned to shoot a gun. But as I approached the time of my pregnancy, it became more and more difficult to face the typewriter. My intentions were good, but day after day I found excuses not to write. If I tried, no words would come.

Finally, I asked for help. I turned to Carl Burak who is my psychiatrist and my friend. He could describe the difficult time and provide the medical information that is so important.

For me, writing or reading about what happened was painful. In a way, however, it was part of my therapy.

No matter how difficult this was, I feel that I had no choice.

—MICHELE G. REMINGTON

# 1

In Vermont, because of the long winter, a psychiatrist's most difficult time coincides with an accountant's most difficult time: the two months prior to April 15. If possible, toward the end of that period, I flee to a warm climate and do nothing. In 1987, Saturday, April 4, was the last full day of my vacation.

The rain in Bennington came down in sheets. I awakened two thousand miles away to the sounds of the ocean. The soft sea breeze stirred the curtains in the room. Ronnie and I, along with good friends, had rented a very simple beach cottage on the island of St. Barthélemy. If you place your finger on the tip of Florida and allow it to slide across the water to Cuba, and then follow the curving archipelago of islands east and south you will come to the Dutch and French island of St. Maarten. If your map shows a small dot just north of St. Maarten, that is probably St. Barthélemy. The ocean is turquoise, the climate serene, the food great, and there are no golf courses or high rises.

Dawn is my favorite time of day. As I awakened at 6:00 A.M., all was quiet. I slipped into a pair of shorts and running shoes and spent the next hour running through the gorgeous scenery, watching the sun rise, watching the ocean, lost in a reverie of good feeling.

The house was still quiet when I returned. I sat on the porch for a while, drawn to the ocean's infinity. I was sorry to see this vacation come to an end. It had been wonderful.

A few thoughts of home wandered through my mind as I sat there. Had the weather turned soft? Probably not—but it wouldn't be too long before spring forced its way into the Green Mountains. Was my desk piled high with messages? Probably. I pushed such thoughts away. By late tomorrow I would be home, time enough for reality.

I heard a noise behind me. I turned to see my friend and colleague, Tom Snyder, carefully opening the screen door carrying a cup of coffee in each hand.

It was probably about that same time that Michele Remington was getting out of bed in Bennington. The morning sky in southern Vermont was dark and brooding as the rain struck her window. The morning sky over the Caribbean was bright as Tom and I enjoyed our coffee.

Sunday evening, April 5

As much as I had loved the week of quiet and beauty, I really missed my son. Eli was one month shy of his ninth birthday, a wonderful age. During the week there had been some very distinct moments of emptiness where his voice would have normally filled the void.

It was a little past his bedtime when we pulled into the driveway. We knew he would be up. Leaving the luggage in the car, Ronnie and I immediately went inside. He came running, arms opened wide.

It couldn't have been more than ten minutes later that the phone rang. Ronnie, Eli, and I were sitting in the kitchen having a snack. My eyes were watching my son as I listened to Dr. Fred Loy, a friend, and one of four surgeons in Bennington. He explained that the day before a young woman, Michele Remington, picked up a .22 caliber pistol and fired two bullets. The first ended the life of her infant son. The second would have ended her own life had she not had surgery. He asked me to see her.

In those first few seconds of understanding there were no thoughts of helping. There I was, in the midst of a reunion with my own child, and I am told that a mother has shot and killed her baby. I'm not sure I can describe or even remember the next moment. It was as though time had come to an abrupt halt. When it started up again I felt angry and ungracious. I expressed my shock. I probably said something like "be glad to help"—but inside I thought "I wish you had called someone else." Maybe in the morning I would tell Fred that I couldn't take the case. I had some soul-searching to do.

I hung up the phone and looked at Eli. Then I went over and hugged him desperately. "Time for bed." He was tired and didn't protest. A few minutes later he was asleep. But I just sat there on the edge of his bed listening to the sound of his life.

# 2

After a few minutes I slipped quietly from Eli's room. I heard Ronnie talking on the phone as I was hauling suitcases upstairs. In the mindlessness of unpacking and sorting laundry I had time to think.

The meaning of Fred Loy's words filled me like water fills a dry sponge. The gods had unleashed an arrow into the exact center of human anguish; not a micron off—an exact bull's-eye. A mother had taken the life of her own child. The thought of trying to help her through this situation seemed overwhelming. Was treatment even an appropriate word?

But there was even more. From what Dr. Loy said, it seemed likely that Mrs. Remington would be prosecuted for murder. My involvement with her would almost inevitably draw me into the morass of the insanity defense, something that I had avoided since graduating from law school.

In the mid-seventies the University of California allowed me to study both law and psychiatry, overlapping my final year of law school and my first year of my psychiatric residency. I received my law degree in 1976 and completed training in psychiatry in 1978. As a law student I had been very interested in the insanity defense but developed some real concern about the psychiatrist's role as an expert in such cases—concerns that I felt very personally that night.

When John Hinckley attempted to assassinate Ronald Reagan, five psychiatrists said "sane," while five others said "insane." If forensic psychiatry were truly objective, truly scientific, how could so many experts differ this way? And to be Michele Remington's treating physician and have to testify (which I knew was inevitable) would be a dilemma. If I felt she had been sane at the time she pulled the trigger, the likely outcome would be a conviction for murder. How could we have a "therapeutic" relationship under those circumstances? On the other hand, if I felt she did not know or understand what she was doing, could I be sure that my "scientific" opinion was not warped by my desire to help her?

I don't think I ever lost a vacation so quickly.

# 3

As I entered the hospital's intensive care unit on Monday morning, I became aware of a man and a woman standing to my left. The man looked to be in his early fifties; the woman a few years younger. They seemed almost huddled together, each supporting the other. In the beginning it was obvious that the woman had been crying, and somehow I knew they were Michele Remington's mother and father, Philip and Helen Cort. I wasn't ready to speak with them just yet. As I continued toward the nursing station in the center of this circular room two nurses approached. The first was Michael Brent, the very competent head nurse who had worked in our intensive care unit for more than ten years. The second was Ellen Goldman, a bright sensitive woman with more than three years' experience in ICU. Both were people whose opinions and perceptions about patients had been very helpful in the past. They knew who I had come to see.

Ellen spoke first. "We didn't know what to expect with Michele—so far she's just been very quiet, almost like she's in a fog." Michael added, "Medically she's stable—everything seems routine. If there's anything we should be doing, let us know." I said 1 would, then Michael added, "It's her parents over there who seem to need the help now"—he nodded his head almost imperceptibly toward the couple I had noticed. Ellen added, "And her husband too—he walks in, doesn't stay long and leaves. I've known Jeff for a long time and I've never seen him like this. I'm worried."

I thanked them both.

I wasn't surprised by what they had said. If Helen and Philip Cort and Jeff Remington hadn't each been in their version of hell I would have thought it abnormal. That Michele seemed to be "in a fog" also seemed understandable.

We all have instinctive ways of protecting ourselves from what is too painful to bear. At the very least a tragedy or loss takes some time to sink in so that we are not struck with the full impact in the beginning. In dire situations we can protect ourselves with even more insulation, blocking out a memory entirely.

The dose of horror, of atrocity, of anguish that causes someone to hide behind unreality or to lose memory is not the same for each person. There is no formula to measure the insult required, but it is almost a mark of our humanness that there is just so much each of us can take. This young woman that I was about to see, lying in a bed just twenty feet away, was dealing with a situation that was untenable. With her own hands she had taken the life of her child. If my heart and gut were right, she would be in pain as long as her life continued.

I glanced at the chart rack and found the one that said REMINGTON on the spine. Pulling it out I reviewed the contents. The last thing I looked at before walking into Michele's room was Dr. Loy's progress note from the day before.

April 5, 1987

Post operative day #1. Patient awake. Vital signs stable. Hematocrit 36%. Hemoglobin 12.7. Electrolytes okay. Chest x-ray—left lung expanded. Abdomen—soft without bowel sounds.

I asked patient if she knew what happened. She said "No." I asked if she remembered yesterday. "It rained."

I explained that she shot herself and needed surgery to stop the bleeding.

I asked her if she remembered her baby. She said "My baby!" I told her she shot her baby. She closed her eyes and cried.

Plan:

Psychiatry consult
Suicide precautions
Supportive care

Signed: F. Loy

I put the chart down. It was time. In the few seconds it took to walk across the carpeted moat of open space between the nursing station and Michele Remington's room, I felt as though I was crossing an invisible dividing line between my previous experiences as a physician and a new territory where the usual rules of the game seemed lame and irrelevant. I felt very alone at that moment and almost frightened—facing a challenge that seemed overwhelming; for the hundredth time in the past twelve hours, I thought to myself, "after what has happened—after what she has done, can I really help her survive—let alone move through the chapters of her future in some meaningful way?"

The room was quiet. The head of Michele's bed was elevated and a plastic bag of intravenous solution hung on her right. I automatically checked to see that it was running properly; a hangover from my days as a family practitioner.

Michele was told that I would be coming to see her. She didn't want to speak to a psychiatrist. She didn't want to speak to anybody. She told me later that she had planned to ask me to leave.

I softly said "Hello" and introduced myself. She said "Hi," also softly. Struggling for the next words I asked if she was in pain. "Some—it's not too bad."

Then Michele looked directly at me. Reflections from her large brown-rimmed glasses prevented me from completely seeing her eyes, but for an instant there was a connection. She decided not to throw me out.

I was struck by Michele's physical weakness. It had been less than forty-eight hours since she had fired a bullet into her chest. In fact, Fred Loy told me that he believed the gun must have been fired while Michele's heart was in systole (while it was contracting); the path of the bullet was such that it probably would have struck her heart had it been in diastole (and therefore expanded). Clearly she had not intended to live. Her life had been spared by millimeters.

That first conversation was understandably brief.

"Dr. Loy asked me to speak with you, to try to understand what happened and to help in any way that I can." Michele was no longer making eye contact but she nodded, giving me permission to continue. She was certainly subdued, obviously unhappy, and definitely uncomfortable, but somehow not as distraught as I expected.

Up to this point I had simply assumed that Michele knew what really happened. Suddenly, I wasn't sure. I knew from Dr. Loy's note that she had been told that she "shot her baby." I would later find out that she had asked her husband about their child and he had replied "Joshua is no longer with us." So it seemed impossible that she wouldn't know, but I felt apprehensive.

I gently asked questions. Yes, she was depressed—had been very depressed for a while. Yes, she had thought about suicide—had even taken some pills the week before. Yes, she remembered the gun. And then nothing. She seemed totally blank about the actual shooting, without one shred of recollection from late morning until after she arrived at the hospital.

I suppose I could have doubted Michele, but I didn't. In fact, right or wrong, I was almost hoping that the protective hole in her memory would continue—at least for a while.

Every life has its own rhythm, its own music, and Michele now had some notes that might never be played. If they were, I felt it had to come from her, not me. I thought for a moment and asked, "Do you understand about your baby?" She nodded. That was all. When I left the room I was still uncertain.

# 4

My name is Michele Remington. I was born in Allentown,
Pennsylvania, in January of 1958, a twin in a family of
five. I have an older sister, Joan, and twin brothers, Robert
and Michael. My (nonidentical) twin sister, Susan, and I are the
youngest. My mother had the five of us in twenty-nine
months!

When I was very small we moved to Smiths Mills, New
Jersey, and lived there until I was fifteen. I truly loved
Smiths Mills, riding bikes along the peaceful roads, exploring
the woods and even enjoying school. It was a wonderful
place to grow up.

In 1972 my father received a job offer that he felt he had
to take. There have been many occasions during these
past twenty years that I have wondered what my life would
have been like if we had stayed in New Jersey, but we
didn't. We moved to Bennington, Vermont. From the
start Vermont seemed difficult. I had to get used to an
environment that didn't easily accept "flatlanders." This
was especially true in school.

I was a freshman in a high school I had never seen
before. In Smiths Mills I had a close group of friends; in
Bennington I knew no one. My twin sister, Susan, was
more attractive and always seemed to have an easier time

with almost anything she wanted. I always wished I were prettier or had a better figure. Now I felt especially plain. God, I was so scared—I missed New Jersey so much.

During most of that first year, other than my sister, I had just one good friend, a girl I met in my art class with whom I became very close. Her family had moved from Pennsylvania and she seemed to understand my feelings. We really needed each other during those "growing up" years.

Although I did not use drugs of any kind, there were two or three occasions during high school when I experimented with marijuana, perhaps trying to gain acceptance. I didn't like it. I also learned that I couldn't handle alcohol very well. The few times that I did drink, I didn't like it, either.

My junior and senior years were a little easier, but I continued to feel that New Jersey was really home. I did, however, manage to make more friends and have my share of teenage crushes and adolescent heartbreaks.

In 1976, immediately after graduation, I was maid of honor at a friend's wedding. This was another way Vermont, or at least Bennington, seemed different than Smiths Mills. So many people in this area marry right after high school, and then later, often after they have children, couples divorce. I vowed this would never happen to me. I wanted to be emotionally ready to take on the responsibility of children and to have a marriage as solid as that of my parents.

I had decided that I would not go to college. I just wasn't interested. I have a modest amount of artistic talent and could've gone to art school, but the best art-related jobs are in the city and I didn't want to live in a city. So I went to work. I bought my first car on Howard Johnson's waitressing tips, moved on to summer work in a local orchard (even painted a few Halloween pumpkins), and then went to work for a local pharmacy. In fact, at the grand opening of the pharmacy I dressed up as Mr. Planter's peanut and dispensed free samples. The kids loved it. One little boy just couldn't stop laughing and called me "a real big nut."

At the time I didn't have specific long-range goals. I just wanted to work and save money to buy the simple things in life. I probably would have been content to try different kinds of jobs for a while had I not received an offer at a new factory that was producing electrical transformers and capacitors. The pay was good but it was actually the medical benefits that attracted me. There has always been a black medical cloud hanging over my head. I seem to become ill easily, and when I do unusual complications often follow. For instance, when I was ten I almost died in a coma following a penicillin reaction, and on another occasion a simple appendectomy was complicated by a postoperative infection.

While I was working at my different jobs, my brother Bob and sister Joan were in college, my twin sister Susan held a full-time job locally, and my brother Michael (Bob's twin) was at the Saratoga Special School in Saratoga, New York.

You see, Michael was brain-damaged at birth, possibly because of a doctor's negligence. My parents have suffered with that burden for years, but they have been strong. They raised him with much love. Things were not easy but they provided us all with a good home.

It was difficult with a brother like Michael; it took a long time to really understand what was wrong with him. Sometimes I felt that maybe in a sense he was luckier than most of us because he didn't have to deal with the pressures of growing up and the frustrations of independence.

*It was also difficult dealing with people who were not
so willing to understand. School kids can be especially cruel
to someone who is different. I think the experience of
helping Michael helped me to be more compassionate toward
people who are not as fortunate as I. All in all, it forced
me to grow up faster.*

*My parents kept Michael at home until he was fifteen, then
they reluctantly made the decision to place him in a
special school in Saratoga, New York, where he would live
and we would visit. It was a very difficult decision but
a necessary one because he needed twenty-four-hour care.
He couldn't read or write or even speak a full sentence.
He would say "mom," "dad," and "Coca-Cola."*

*I noticed on my first few visits to see him at school that
there were always several other kids who would hug you
and try to spend time with you. After talking with the staff
I found that these kids and many others like them were
as good as abandoned. Their parents visited rarely or never.
If anything, this realization strengthened the love and
respect I felt for my own mother and father. They are special.*

# 5

Jeff is my husband. His courage during these past few years
has amazed me. In the beginning, after Joshua's death, I
expected him to leave. At times I almost wanted him to go
so I would be punished more. Now, I am just grateful
that we still have each other.

I had known Jeff in high school, but our relationship did
not really begin until I attempted to fix him up with a
friend of mine at Southern Vermont College. She backed out
at the last moment so I went instead. It was a great
evening and I found myself wanting to spend time with him.

Jeff worked for his father maintaining apartments that his
father owned. Multitalented, with magical hands, he is
inventive and can fix just about anything. He can do almost
any kind of carpentry, plumbing, or electrical work.

Eventually Jeff and I decided to live together in an
enormous old Victorian house that his father owned. The
house had been divided into seven apartments and Jeff had
the smallest one in the back of the building. We lived in
that apartment for three months while Jeff converted most
of the building into a dormitory for Southern Vermont
College, and also developed a "penthouse" apartment for us
on the third floor. When it was ready we moved in.

We loved it there and made it our home for three years.

Eventually, however, we grew tired of being unofficial dorm parents. Most of the time this was fun, but trying to keep the place in one piece and keeping a lid on the rowdy parties was not easy.

We decided to move; we also decided to marry. The date would be October 3, 1981. I planned a candlelight ceremony. The wedding party would include my two sisters and Jeff's three brothers. We wrote our own wedding vows, which expressed our very special love and commitment.

I knew this would be a good marriage and that no matter what life dealt us, we would get through it. I felt this way because we were able to really talk with one another. Some of the time we would talk into the wee small hours. There wasn't much we couldn't discuss. Even if we were not able to solve a problem or make it go away, each of us was willing to listen.

On the evening of our wedding as we came down the long hallway stairs, the entire house of resident college students was waiting at the bottom to congratulate us. It was a nice gesture and we knew that they cared about us, but we also knew that our wedding gave them an excuse to throw another party!

While we lived in our penthouse Jeff's father bought a motel. At first Jeff's brother and his wife lived there and managed the operation, but they had five children and found that it wasn't working out. We were asked if we'd like to take over and we decided to give it a try.

The motel was beautiful. A long driveway led up to twenty units that sat on a hill overlooking a valley. The lawn was spacious, with an in-ground pool. The house in which we would live was closer to the road and attached to the office. At the time we moved to the motel, we decided to invest in real estate ourselves. We bought two houses, *which had a total of seven apartments. Unfortunately, the apartments were in desperate need of attention. As landlords and motel managers we really had our hands full.*

*Not long after we bought the apartments, on a bitter cold day in January, which happened to be my birthday, the larger of the two houses caught fire. Because there were people living there who were put out of their home, I was devastated. Fortunately, no one was hurt.*

*The fire actually proved to be a blessing in disguise. At the rate we were going it would have taken us twenty years to rehabilitate; after the fire it was done in a matter of months. In a short time the problems of being a decent landlord resumed.*

*That year around Christmas Jeff and some of his friends were at the Montgomery Ward Catalog Store and they saw pictures of puppies that were being given away. They were so adorable that no one could resist. Jeff got the last one. Later that day, when I returned home after shopping, I found this cute puppy on the couch. She was half Beagle and half Basset Hound. The men had been sitting around the living room watching football and drinking Old Milwaukee beer, and that's what they named her—"Old Milwaukee." We called her "Millie" for short.*

*Millie became a surrogate child, but our parental instincts were not satisfied. A few months later we found a cat under the motel. He had been there at least three days after suffering with a dislocated hip. We named him Arthur. We took him to a vet and he had surgery. While Arthur was recovering he and Millie really hit it off. Sometimes we would turn off the TV and watch them instead, they were so amusing.*

*It was about that time that I went out with Jeff behind the motel and learned to shoot a gun. Jeff had a few rifles and one pistol. He wanted me to learn to shoot for self-*

defense, and it wasn't such a bad idea. The motel sat all alone on twelve acres of land; sometimes it was very dark and quiet. It was a public business, anyone could walk in, and occasionally I met some pretty strange characters, I was often nervous at night, especially when Jeff was not home.

I didn't think I could handle a big gun, but I had seen a friend of mine practice with a small pistol and decided that I might be able to handle that. So that's what Jeff got. I did learn how to shoot but I didn't like it. I went out to practice a few times and then I put the gun away. I kind of forgot about it.

# 6 🍂

When Jeff's dad became interested in selling the motel we began to look for a house. We had become a little spoiled and did not want to go back to apartment living. We were also planning to start a family and felt that this was the time to establish a more permanent home.

At first we thought about buying, but very quickly our dreams changed to building on our own. Jeff was able to handle everything from start to finish, and we decided we would look for land. We wanted enough space to protect us from someone else building too close. We wanted to look out of our windows and see woods and mountains instead of someone's living room.

We were incredibly lucky. We quickly found land for sale just three or four miles out of town, next to an apple orchard. There was a gorgeous view of mountains to the south. One particular piece was perfect for us. It consisted of about five acres of open fields and five acres of woods. I knew people who had paid $10,000 for one acre; we bought our ten acres for $14,000.

The sale of the motel happened much sooner than we expected. For a while, before we finished building, we would have to move into one of our own apartments. We

weren't enthusiastic but accepted this minor sacrifice
because the house of our dreams was in sight.

Everything seemed fine. We were happy and content. Millie
and Arthur were thriving and we felt we were ready to
be parents.

It was a beautiful June day when my pregnancy test came
back positive. I was beside myself with joy. I couldn't
wait to share the news with Jeff, but he was on a construction
site in New York State and usually did not get home until
dusk. I waited.

I was smiling from ear to ear when Jeff walked through
the door. I handed him a cigar that I had bought that
afternoon. He looked back and forth between the cigar and
my smile for a few seconds and then let out a yell—we
were ecstatic!

The next day was Saturday, but Jeff did not work as he
often does. Instead we took a picnic lunch to the land we
had just purchased. All day we walked and hugged and
talked.

A decision we made that day will probably haunt me
forever. Jeff and I discussed doctors. I really wanted to
continue with Dr. Robert Benjamin, whom I had been seeing.
I instinctively trusted him and knew he was a caring
person. But the baby would be born in mid-February and we
were in snow country. Dr. Benjamin's office was in
Williamstown, Massachusetts, only twenty minutes away,
but he delivered babies in the North Adams,
Massachusetts, hospital, which was about a forty-five-
minute trip. Going over the mountain in winter could be
treacherous. Jeff often worked some distance away, and even
though he could try to get home quickly, it might not be
quick enough.

So there was a real chance that I would have to drive

myself to the hospital (of course, I could have asked someone else, but I wasn't likely to do that). I had a hunch that I was not going to be too mobile in my ninth month. The hospital in Bennington was only five minutes away, and it just didn't make sense to go to North Adams. I was very upset. I felt rotten about changing doctors, but at the same time it seemed as though that was the only rational thing to do. Bennington had three obstetricians. I was told that Dr. Kevin Murray was good and I made an appointment.

From the first, it just wasn't like being with Dr. Benjamin. Dr. Murray was nice enough, but his office was jammed and I always felt as though I had to rush. He didn't seem to have time to listen. Of course it's easy enough now to ask myself why I didn't follow my instinct and go back to Dr. Benjamin, but the truth is—there was nothing really wrong. It just didn't seem as "right."

# 7

Pregnancy was exciting but not physically comfortable. During the first four months I had morning sickness, only it wasn't always confined to the morning. I was constantly nauseous and had frequent headaches. Even later, when I wasn't nauseous, I did not have a real appetite. Most of the time I had to force myself to eat.

Going to work became more difficult. The work itself was fine but I objected to the gossiping, which was rampant. My "problem" was that I refused to discuss any personal business, as so many of the other women seemed to do so freely. The grapevine was fast. Any juicy bit of information mentioned in the morning was known throughout the building by afternoon.

I had been brought up to feel that somebody else's business was their business, and therefore I refused to be part of the grapevine. I did not speak about somebody else's troubles. If someone bothered me I let them know about it. I was probably not very popular, but I did have a group of good friends at work and any free time I had I spent with them. With the exception of a very few ladies who I tried to absolutely avoid, most of the time I just tried to be civil. That was before my pregnancy.

The bitchiness and backbiting, which I objected to before

*my pregnancy, really got to me during my first trimester.
I doubt the ladies had changed, I was just intolerant (and
maybe a bit intolerable myself). I missed more work days
than ever before and tried to build a shell around myself
while I was there. Sometimes I just ignored people; at
other times I was downright rude. Outspoken is normal for
me; rude is not.*

*Toward the end of my first trimester I was ready to quit.
Realizing, however, that I felt a little better in the evening
than during the day, I switched to the 4:00 P.M.-to-midnight
shift in September and also to an entirely different
department.*

*I soon felt much better. I'm not sure whether the
improvement was caused by the lessening of my morning
sickness, which occurred at about that time,
or the change in my work circumstances, or both, but
suddenly everything fell into place. In my new
department everyone seemed more laid-back, less prone to
gossip, and more genuine about their feelings for each
other.*

*At first Jeff was not happy about the change in my schedule.
We had a very limited amount of time together. I would
leave by quarter of four; he would come home at five or six.
Sometimes he stayed up till I came home; at other times
I would find him asleep.*

*Our weekend time became more important. Slowly we got
used to the limitations. Besides, when the baby came and
I was back at work we would only need a sitter for a few
hours each day.*

*My middle trimester was tolerable. Physically I didn't feel
great, but I was not downright sick as I had been. My
third trimester, however, was terrible. In November Jeff
began to work on our new home. I would normally have
helped but I was just too uncomfortable. I was into my*

seventh month and beginning to retain fluid in my legs.
At work I had to take more and more breaks.

My boss did everything she could to make the job more
comfortable. I wore surgical socks and eliminated salt,
but no matter what I did my weight shot up and the fluid
retention became dramatic.

There were quite a few days when I had to leave work
because my feet and ankles were too swollen. The only
thing I could do was to go home, lie down, and elevate my
feet. One night the swelling was so extreme I became
frightened. Jeff measured the circumference of my ankles—
they were fourteen inches around!

Dr. Murray was concerned about phlebitis and he referred
me to a vascular specialist to see if I had any deep blood
clots. At the time I didn't but I was instructed to stay on
my back with my legs up as much as possible. Ten
minutes on my feet, however, and the swelling returned. I
was very worried. Phlebitis scared me. I had known a
woman who was hospitalized several times because of it and
I didn't want any part of that.

I was due on Valentine's Day and wanted to work until
the end of January in order to be able to take more time
off after the baby was born (the company's rules about
maternity leave were fairly strict). Midway into
December, however, it was evident that I was not
going to make it. I was fat and unbearably swollen. My
attendance at work was slipping. I fought the inevitable
as long as possible, knowing I would go stir-crazy if I had
to stay at home with little to do. I hung on until January
5, but that was it. It was downhill from that time on.

For a few weeks I managed to find things to do, but day
by day chores were becoming more difficult. At the time,
having left the motel, we were living in one of our own third-
floor walkups while Jeff continued to work on our new

home. The multiple flights of stairs became harder and harder to climb. Walking Millie was the hardest of all. She had to be taken out at least twice a day and couldn't run free——Bennington has a leash law.

One of our tenants in the building was a family of five. Two of the children were teenagers and the younger child was nine. They were all terrific. We liked each other very much and the kids were always coming up to visit. The more I needed help, the more they did.

I am the type of person who prefers doing things for myself, so accepting this help was difficult. By that point my mother had begun to make daily visits and that I couldn't stop, but I did everything to sneak by the kids and not impose on them. On a few occasions they caught me trying to lug bags of groceries up the stairs. They gave me cain. Eventually it became so difficult that I gave in and whenever I'd ask for help they'd never hesitate. They took Millie for walks several times a day, went grocery shopping, and even cleaned. I don't know what I would have done without them.

They seemed especially interested in my pregnancy. We would sit on the porch and talk for a long time about all my expectations. I would show them every new item of baby clothing that I bought. I was excited and the enthusiasm was growing. It was only much later, in the aftermath of the tragedy, that I learned how upset the children had been with my physical and emotional deterioration during the last two months of my pregnancy.

I had really begun to gain weight. I mean really. At delivery I would pack 210 pounds on my 5'2" frame. Fluid retention was terrible. An ultrasound two weeks prior to delivery suggested that the baby would weigh at least nine pounds.

I was never comfortable. I couldn't sit in a chair for more than half an hour before I started to fidget. I could only sleep on my side, and I would constantly switch from right to left. My stomach was so huge that I couldn't sit comfortably at a table. When I bathed, Jeff had to wash my feet because I couldn't reach them. I outgrew all my shoes. At night, between my need to go to the bathroom and my heartburn, I slept poorly. I tried everything——took antacids, drank warm water, and ate celery, but two hours of sleep was the most I could get at any one time. Eventually, because of my restlessness, Jeff had to sleep in the other room.

Those last two months seemed like two years. I could no longer drive a car, literally unable to fit behind the steering wheel and still reach the pedals. I was agitated, sleep deprived, irritable, uncomfortable, totally fat, tired of being cooped up, and unable to think of anything but "the big day."

I had been reading all kinds of books and literature on pregnancy. I thought that all I was experiencing and all my feelings were normal. Perhaps extreme, but normal. I knew that the discomfort would not last forever, and when I had the baby in my arms all of the misery would be worth it. My friends were telling me that excessive heartburn meant either a boy or a baby with a lot of hair. Both would be fine with me, but most of all I wanted a healthy child.

I was the first of my brothers and sisters to be married, and now I was the first to be pregnant. Jeff's parents already had six grandchildren. For my parents, this would be their first. There was so much to look forward to.

Jeff loved the idea of being a dad, and even with my difficulties I had no doubts about motherhood. Ellen, one of my best friends, had two little girls, Rebecca and Marsha. Often they would stay with me for a night or two when their parents had to be away. I never forgot their birthdays or Christmas. I loved them as if they were my own. Sue, another friend, had a little boy whose name was Michael. I've known him since he was born and he's always been "my special guy." I have six nieces and nephews who were always visiting. I was always around kids. I loved them and was good with them. I had no doubts that I would be a good mother.

Christmas of 1986 passed, and so did my twenty-ninth birthday. At about that time my mother and my dear friend, Barbara, had a baby shower for me. I received many beautiful things, but the best present of all was an absolutely breathtaking hand-made wooden cradle that came wrapped in a huge red ribbon. It was up on a stand so that bending was minimal. Inside, the bedding and pillows had been made by my sisters.

My entire family had gotten together and commissioned a local craftsman to make that cradle. It was physically the most beautiful gift I had ever received, but more than that I cherished it because it was a gift of the heart.

# 8 ⟜

We approached Valentine's Day, my due date, with great anticipation. Our childbirth classes were finished and we were ready. But February 14 came and went. A week passed, and then ten days. Both of us were frustrated. Jeff was working almost two hours from home and he was reluctant to leave, afraid that I would go into labor while he was away. I tried to assure him that he would be able to get home in time.

At three-thirty on the morning of February 23 I realized that my membranes had ruptured. I noticed some blood and knew I should go to the hospital immediately, but I was not having pain and did not want to disturb Jeff. His alarm was set early, so I just waited.

When I look back on those few hours I realize how "out of it" I felt. I sat quietly in my bathroom in a fog. It was as though my real self was inside some kind of unbreakable outer layer, and I had the sense that no one could really hear me if I spoke. This feeling seemed to get even more intense as the events of labor and delivery unfolded.

We made contact with Dr. Murray's office at eight in the morning. At first his nurse suggested that I come to the office at nine, but when I explained that fluid would flow every time I stood up and I was certain that my

membranes had ruptured, she instructed me to go directly
to the hospital.

As soon as I arrived at the hospital, I was admitted and
confined to bed. I was also hooked up to a fetal monitor,
which had to be repositioned every time I switched sides.

I had done some reading and was aware that the first
pregnancy is often followed by a long labor. I had a hunch
that my labor would last about twenty hours, but I didn't
understand just how long that could be.

As time went by Jeff refused to leave my side, so I
asked a friend of ours who is a nurse to take him to the
cafeteria and make sure he ate. I settled into a long
winter's day and night.

More hours passed. Dr. Murray came by after his office
hours were finished, but I was still in the first stage of
labor. I was having contractions, but very little pain, nothing
more than I had experienced with my monthly cramps.
In fact, the nurses seemed surprised that I was dozing off
while the monitor showed I was having large
contractions.

At midnight, almost twenty hours after my membranes
had ruptured, I was still in the labor room. I hadn't eaten
solid food for almost thirty hours. Fluids were restricted and
the snatches of sleep I did get were very brief. I was tired
and increasingly afraid.

Although they told me not to worry, I felt something was
wrong. For most of the day the baby's heartbeat was
slowing when I had contractions. I was told that they were
"watching it closely," and they even showed me tapes
from the fetal monitor. I trusted the staff and tried
to believe it must be okay, but I wasn't completely reassured.
A month earlier, when Dr. Murray said how large the
baby was, he told me he wasn't sure I could deliver vaginally.

Sometime during the evening Dr. Murray explained that

he was going to assist labor or do a C-section if I made no progress by 2:00 A.M. I was so spent, so tired, so worried that the baby was just too big, that I wanted him to do the C-section right then and get it over with.

The night dragged on. 2:00 A.M. came and went. Nothing happened. My progress was very slow. I'll never know for sure, but I believe that Dr. Murray would have done the C-section if the clock had been turned back a year.

In the months before my delivery the local newspaper had reported that the doctors in Bennington had been doing more C-sections than any other doctors in the state of Vermont. There was a great deal of discussion about unnecessary surgery and the need for second opinions. I can't help but feel that Dr. Murray was influenced by this and reluctant to do the C-section at that time, unless it was absolutely necessary.

Apparently he had been sleeping down the hall and that night I was the only woman in labor. I'm not sure what time it was when he came in to do the last internal exam, but it hurt like hell. I remember seeing orange fluid run off the side of the table. I saw the calm expression on Dr. Murray's face vanish.

# 9 🍂

Helen Cort was suddenly awake for the third time. She had a sense of foreboding, which for a few seconds she didn't understand, then her mind cleared. Michele.

The house was freezing. The clock read 4:45 A.M. Still no call from the hospital. She slipped from the warm covers, trying not to disturb Philip. Normally the heat would come on automatically at five-fifteen to warm the house before she and Philip got up.

Walking to the kitchen it seemed even colder. Through the large windows above the sink there was no hint of dawn; overhead the sky was filled with stars. Turning on the light, she saw that the thermometer outside the window read fourteen degrees. Inside, the thermostat read fifty-four. Helen pushed the lever to the "manual" position and within seconds heard the furnace come to life.

As Helen Cort stood there on the morning of February 24, she shivered, but it was not from the cold. As the hours of her daughter's labor grew longer, joyous anticipation of the arrival of her first grandchild had given way to a growing apprehension and now to an uncontrollable dread. "God, don't do this again," she pleaded in her thoughts. But she knew. In her heart she knew. Mother and daughter.

"Oh, my God," she whispered to the empty room, to the perking coffeemaker, "Oh, my God." Quietly she began to cry. Thoughts of Kingston, New York, were vivid, crueler than they had been for more than thirty years.


October 13, 1956, was a gorgeous fall day in Kingston, but lying in her hospital bed twenty-three-year-old Helen Cort hadn't noticed. She had been in labor for more than forty hours and was exhausted. Her unborn twins were refusing to make their appearance. She had not had this sort of difficulty fifteen months earlier when her first child Joan was born. She was not destined to have difficulty fourteen months later when a second set of twins, Michele and Susan, would be born. But this was terrible. She knew Philip was very worried, but Dr. McBride would say little to them.

At about ten in the morning Dr. McBride examined her for what seemed to be the hundredth time. Finally, he called Philip back into the room. "We have problems," he said. "It's too late to deliver the twins by Caesarean section." They both wondered why this hadn't been done earlier, but in those moments of tension, Helen and Philip said nothing. "We'll need to use forceps for the first baby and it looks as though the second baby is a breech."

Robert came first, small (four pounds fifteen ounces) but vigorous. Whether it was the stress of the prolonged labor and the trauma of the delivery, or something congenital, his three-pound-eight-ounce brother Michael was never normal.

"It can't be," she whispered to the still empty room, but in her heart she was afraid. The tears just continued down her face.

# 10 🪶

"Dr. Blum, this is Jane Brent at the hospital, I think we've got a real problem here."

Dr. Robert Blum, chief of pediatrics, was immediately awake. Jane was a very experienced pediatric nurse and she didn't make such statements lightly. He looked at the clock, 6:05 A.M.

"What's going on?"

"Kevin Murray asked me to call you. We have a thirty-year-old primigravida who's been in labor for more than twenty-five hours. Early ruptured membranes—variable decelerations noted as early as yesterday afternoon—some absence of beat-to-beat variability—and bloody amniotic fluid—I'll bet it's a partial abruption."

"How big is the baby?"

"Over nine pounds."

"Is the mother a big woman?"

"No—the pelvis is marginal. Vaginal delivery will be difficult. This may turn into a C-section."

What Jane was reporting was disturbing. The fetal heart rate should change slightly from moment to moment, but this baby's did not have "beat-to-beat variability." Also, when contractions occur, the fetal heart rate should remain relatively stable, not dip, or decelerate, as Jane had said.

Dr. Blum agreed that a partial abruption was likely. The placenta attaches to the wall of the uterus and provides the fetus with its blood supply. If the placenta completely tears from the wall of the womb before the baby is born, it is a medical emergency for both infant and mother. A small, partial abruption is not necessarily a cause for urgent action, but it does demand careful attention.

"Damn," is all Bob Blum said. "I'll be right there."

Eleven minutes later Dr. Blum arrived at the hospital. In five minutes he was scrubbed and in the operating room. By the time he had arrived, Michele had received a spinal anesthetic but she looked less than rested. He noted the double setup, two separate intravenous lines connected, one to each arm. This is done whenever there is a threat of sudden excessive blood loss and rapid transfusion or fluid replacement might be crucial.

Everyone in the operating room looked pressured. Jeff Remington had understandably been excluded. As soon as Dr. Blum arrived, Dr. Murray did a midline episiotomy (a midline incision in the perineum routinely done to prevent uncontrolled lacerations as a baby's head is delivered) and applied forceps.

Elise Fender had been an obstetrical nurse for years; she knew the drill. As Dr. Murray applied traction with the forceps she gently pushed on Michele's abdomen.

On the third try the head was extracted, followed quickly and easily by the left shoulder, then the right, then the baby was out. Trouble. The infant was flaccid and gray. There were no spontaneous attempts at breathing. Immediately after the cord was clamped and cut Dr. Murray handed the baby to Dr. Blum.

A minute passed. Michele sensed the urgency in the room and became aware there was no cry. She had not seen or touched her baby; she didn't know if it was a boy or a girl. She was frantic. "What's wrong?" she pleaded. "Can I see my baby?"

For a few seconds there was no reply. At that moment Bob Blum and Jane Brent were removing the baby from the operating room. Elise Fender turned and gently said, "Michele, the baby needs medical attention and has been taken to the nursery." Michele turned her head and bit her lip. Her worst fears, the worst fears of many expectant mothers, were coming true. Something was very wrong.

The baby did not spontaneously breathe. He was covered with meconium, fecal material that is often expelled when the fetus is distressed. Dr. Blum's heart was in his mouth. No matter how many deliveries he attended, no matter how many infants he had helped, when a newborn wouldn't breathe, fear gripped him like a claw. To watch him, however, you wouldn't know it.

Immediately the baby's nose and mouth were covered by an oxygen mask and a breathing bag. At 6:58 A.M., just three minutes after Joshua entered the world, Dr. Blum intubated the baby and immediately suctioned a small amount of bloody meconium-stained fluid from Joshua's airway.

The few weak respiratory efforts that Joshua had made to that point became stronger. His color improved. Five minutes after the breathing tube was placed, it was removed. He was breathing on his own but all was not well.

The baby began to shake. This was more than the usual newborn irritability. He was having small seizures. Dr. Blum was immediately on the phone with the Albany Medical Center where he had trained. They had an excellent neonatal intensive care unit.

Helicopter time between the Southwestern Vermont Medical Center in Bennington and the Albany Medical Center is about twenty-two minutes. Less than an hour after he was born, Joshua Remington was in the air.

# 11 ⚜

The fear was that Joshua had suffered brain damage from
poor cerebral blood circulation at the time of delivery.
Jeff told me that the doctors in Albany could not say how
everything would turn out, but they were hopeful because
infants are so resilient. I don't remember thinking much
about my brother Michael, but I know that was probably
because it was too scary.

The medical staff in Albany were going day by day and
wouldn't tell us exactly when Joshua would be able to
come home, but the word was hopeful. He had to take
phenobarbital to prevent seizures, but otherwise was
doing okay.

I needed time. I didn't feel really ready to have Josh at
home. My experiences with the children of my friends
and family had always seemed very natural, yet I was
actually terrified of my own son. I was afraid I wouldn't
know what to do. Watching the other women nursing their
newborns made me feel even more different, even less
like a mother.

In convincing me that it was okay to leave the hospital,
the maternity nurses assured me that Joshua wouldn't
come directly home. They said that a newborn who went to
Albany would automatically come back to our hospital

*for a week of observation. I almost had them put that in
writing; I had to be convinced that that was the way it
would happen.*

*I was discharged from the hospital on Monday, March 2.
The next day I went to visit Josh for the first time and I
was very nervous. Albany Medical Center seemed confusing
and I was so glad that Jeff knew his way around. When
we arrived in pediatrics I felt almost numb. One of the nurses
approached us holding Joshua in her arms. She asked me
if I'd like to hold him. I looked at Jeff. He was beaming. "Go
on, honey, hold your son."*

*I felt almost paralyzed. Mechanically, like a robot, I held
out my arms. I was holding Joshua just as I had held
many other infants, but there was no joy. I tried to act the
part of the happy mother, but I was terrified.*

*After we were back home I tried to explain to Jeff how I
felt. He didn't seem to understand—almost seemed
irritated that I felt the way I did. All I could think of was
bonding. Bonding, bonding, bonding. Somehow that's
what I had lost because Joshua was taken away and somehow
I had to "catch up."*

*Two days later, on Thursday, we made our second trip to
Albany. Jeff's father again drove us. I didn't feel up to
driving there and Jeff still couldn't drive. He had lost his
license for three years as a result of an accident he'd had
after drinking. In fact, driving me to the hospital for the
delivery was the only driving he had done for a long
timeand he still had a few months to go before getting it
back.*

*The second trip went a little better than the first. I noticed
that Joshua looked much bigger and stronger than the
other newborns, but I was still nervous, still afraid, and still
strangely detached. I was secretly glad that he was in the
hospital and relieved that he would be spending another*

week in the hospital in Bennington before he actually
came home. I needed that time.

The very next morning we got a call from Albany. "Come
and get your son." The day before, during our visit, even
the possibility of discharge was not raised. I asked, "Does
this mean he will be going to the hospital in Bennington?"

"No—you can take him right home."

Jeff was ecstatic. I was confused. Despite my fears and my
need for time, leaving Joshua in the hospital the day before
had not been easy, but the idea of suddenly having him at
home full time felt overwhelming.

For the third time Jeff called his father who said he would
be happy to take us to Albany. I wanted to tell my mother
the news. I called her repeatedly but the line remained busy.
Finally I called my father at work and explained the
situation. I asked him to call mom as soon as possible and
let her know. I also asked that he and mom wait until
the next day to visit. I was feeling very nervous and just
wanted a little time to adjust, to be at home alone with
Jeff and Josh for the first time. Maybe it was wrong of me to
ask that, but it didn't seem like a big deal at the time. Dad
said that was fine—he would tell mom. We drove over to
Jeff's parents' house and his dad drove from there.

The trip went smoothly; Joshua seemed fine. He was
probably a little sleepy from his medication and he
napped most of the way home. When we arrived at the
Remingtons' to switch cars, Joshua woke up. He began
to scream.

I was very upset because I didn't know what to do with
him, how to get him to stop crying. Then I remembered
that someone had told me the first day you bring a baby
home is often difficult. I figured it would be twice as hard
for Josh because he had spent so much time in the hospital.
I decided I would have to be patient and just deal with

it, but by the time we arrived at our apartment my nerves were frazzled.

As we drove down the street I saw my mother's gray Chevrolet parked in front of our house. She was in the car and she seemed to be glaring at me and I knew something was wrong. I glanced at Jeff, knowing what his reaction would be. My heart sank.

Jeff and mom were like oil and water. He thought she interfered too much in our business, while I felt she was mostly concerned and interested.

From day one she had been critical of Jeff, rarely saying anything positive, always getting in her digs. Some of this undoubtedly had to do with his drinking, but he had changed. Still, I often found myself defending him and feeling like the monkey in the middle.

Tensions had grown in the past few months. During my last trimester when I was so sick and so down she came over every day to help. I appreciated that even though sometimes I just wanted to be alone. Jeff, however, didn't appreciate it. Too often he would get home and she would still be there. He wanted me to say something to her, and sometimes I felt the same way but I just couldn't. I thought it would hurt her feelings; she could be very sensitive. Meanwhile she would make these comments implying that Jeff wasn't doing enough to help me. Now, with our screaming baby home for the first time in his life, with me feeling terribly inadequate to deal with him, I had an angry husband and a glaring mother to deal with. I just wanted to cry.

I motioned for mom to come out of the car and come inside, which she did. Jeff was steaming but said nothing. She usually didn't criticize Jeff to his face but that day she let loose. I don't remember exactly what she said but she was very angry. She seemed to feel that I had tried to avoid letting her know that the baby was coming home, and she put most of the blame on Jeff.

In response to her yelling, Joshua began screaming louder. My mother was not listening to anything I said in trying to explain what happened, trying to appease her so that her feelings wouldn't be hurt. Jeff was standing on the other side of me and I could feel him reaching his boiling point. At that moment I wanted to run away. Through the noise I suddenly heard Jeff's enraged voice. "Your mother has to leave—now!"

Before I knew what was happening he reached out and grabbed her arm. Mom looked horrified and terrified. I couldn't believe it and I didn't know what Jeff was going to do. He had never done anything like this. He was yelling at her to get out. I stepped between them and began screaming, "What are you doing! What is happening!"

Joshua was having a fit. Jeff let go and walked away. My mother began to cry. The gulf between two of the most important people in my world had become as wide as the Grand Canyon and I was in the middle, with my very upset baby, feeling very much alone.

# 12 🪶

Selma Wright is one of the kindest nurses I have ever met. Graying and quite heavy, this lovely woman has provided young mothers with guidance and good feelings for years. I wasn't surprised when she approached me in the coffee shop. She had been taking care of Michele in maternity just six weeks earlier.

"Hi, Selma."

"Hi, Carl. Could we talk for a few minutes? It's about Michele. I know you can't say too much to me, but I feel so horrible, I can't tell you." She hesitated. "There are some things that may be important."

"Sure," I said, motioning to an empty booth.

As Selma sat down her face became red and tears filled her eyes. I took a napkin and handed it to her. I couldn't remember ever having seen Selma cry. She was always smiling.

"Thanks," She said as she dabbed her face. "You know, the worst part is that we all from the start felt that something wasn't right. But I've had so many young mothers who were struggling, and nothing like this ever happened in all my years of nursing."

"Was there anything about Michele that was different from these other women?"

"Well, it's so hard to say. In a way we were almost expecting Michele to have a difficult time. We were prepared."

"Because of the difficult delivery?"

"Well, that's part of it—you know, I wasn't in the delivery room with her but from what I understand it was tense. Jane Brent told me that the baby was in real trouble." Selma paused. "Maybe to you this won't sound silly, but I think things might have been different if Michele had had a chance to hold or at least to have seen her son in the delivery room."

"She didn't?"

"No. You know it's real unusual in this day and age for a mother not to get a chance to see her baby but that's what happened to Michele. She was stuck in delivery. Kevin was doing major repair work on her lacerations—real bad by the way—and that poor baby was whisked to Albany before she even saw him."

Selma continued, "I've been around here for so long I can remember when we used to take all C-section babies to the nursery immediately because they were more prone to early respiratory problems. We took them out so we could watch them closely—the mothers would have to wait." Selma smiled then for the first time. "Well—sometimes I cheated a little bit and let a few mothers hold their baby, but generally that's what we did for years. Now, unless there's an obvious problem, C-section babies are given to their mothers immediately. In fact, even if there is an urgent medical problem, if at all possible we find a way to get mother and baby together."

Selma must have seen a look on my face.

"I'm not saying that just because she didn't see or touch her baby early on that all of this happened, but I think it was unfortunate."

I nodded. Bonding is very important, but this situation was not the result of only one cause. So many pieces were a part of this puzzle—and I appreciated knowing as much as possible.

"I agree, Selma, I think it is important—so is that why you expected trouble with Michele?"

"That and the fact that she wouldn't go to Albany."

"You mean to visit Josh?"

"No—she was offered the opportunity to be transferred there but she said no. Over the years we've had a number of occasions when newborns have been transferred to Albany. Usually we make arrangements to transfer the mother as well so she can be with her baby. We offered this to Michele on a few occasions but she wouldn't go. We were more and more worried. It is difficult to describe just how you know that a mother who seems reasonable and rational is really suffering and scared, but after years in this business somehow you do. Every day Jeff would go to Albany and return. Michele would express interest in Joshua's condition, but something was just not right. She tried to be concerned but somehow she seemed detached and maybe even frightened."

"Selma, did anyone think about calling me or Don or Peter for a psychiatric consult?"

"A few of us mentioned it. I'm not sure if it ever got to Dr. Murray, and obviously he didn't. But I do know that Maureen Dennis [director of social services] did suggest it when she spoke to Jeff and Michele a few days after Joshua was born. Maureen was very worried that they both were overly optimistic about Josh's condition. That's not so unusual of course. Most parents want to feel that everything with their child will be okay, but Maureen felt like we did—that something was just not right."

"But nothing came of her suggestion?" It was more of a statement than a question.

"From what Maureen told me, it was Jeff who wouldn't consider it."


The first thing you should know about Jeff Remington is that he no longer drinks. He stopped about two years before Joshua was born. Throughout the entire ordeal he touched not one drop.

Jeff saw the light one cold rainy night when, driving drunk, he lost control of his Jeep and somehow fell out of the doorless vehicle. Lying on the wet roadway he watched the scene as if it were in slow motion; the Jeep spun and crashed into a wall with three of his inebriated friends. Miraculously, no one was seriously injured, but Jeff knew it was just luck. He could have been responsible for three deaths.

Fully intending never to drink again, by noon of the next day Jeff was in trouble. He knew he needed help and was admitted to a rehabilitation program. He completed twenty-five of the twenty-eight days in the program and then, deciding that he was finished, he quit.

Most people who stay twenty-five days would complete the program. Most individuals who successfully stop drinking attend AA (Alcoholics Anonymous). He didn't. Many people continue with counseling after their alcohol rehabilitation. He didn't. He just never drank again. Jeff Remington can be very stubborn. Sometimes this serves him well; sometimes it doesn't.

Ruggedly handsome, Jeff was waiting for me when I left Michele that first day. Tears were running down his cheeks as he stood outside of her intensive care room.

We found a separate room, one that was quiet and private, and sat facing one another. Light from the totally gray sky was streaming in from a side window and added to his pallor—he looked like a ghost.

"I'm so sorry, Jeff."

He tried to say something but just shrugged and nodded his head. He was still struggling to choke back the tears.

"Can you help her?" he finally said.

"I'll try—I'll help both of you in any way I can." He didn't say anything for a few seconds, then looked at me with his red tearful eyes and blurted, "I can be so damned bullheaded sometimes—so stubborn. The nurses told me right in the beginning, six weeks ago, that Michele should get counseling. I said no, 'If you have a problem you should stand on your own two feet and deal with it,' that's what I said. Real smart, huh, doc?" I didn't have to answer; Jeff just continued to pour out his guilt. "Even Helen, Michele's mother"—he paused—"who I don't get along with, tried to get help for her, and I just dug in my heels. Didn't do a damn thing." Jeff's eyes dropped to the floor.

I waited for a few moments and then said softly, "Hindsight is always easy."

Jeff nodded, but his eyes remained glued to the rug. I noticed a few tears drop and create wet spots. There was a box of always available hospital tissues on the table next to him. I reached over and handed him the box. He pulled out a few sheets and dried his cheeks.

I waited a few moments and then said, "It might help me to understand if you could tell me what Michele was like these past few weeks."

He looked up. "Well, I realize she wasn't right—so reluctant to take care of Joshua, almost as if she were afraid. She couldn't really do much, she would just sit and rock sometimes. But I figured she would come out of it. She had a real tough few months at the end of her pregnancy. Her labor and delivery were hell on wheels, and then on top of it Josh went to Albany."

"So in a way her behavior sort of made sense to you?"

"Yeah. I guess in a way it did." He shook his head, and tears were again filling his lower lids. As they began to flow down his face he looked toward the window for a few seconds. I think I shuddered. It was difficult to watch his pain at that moment.

Jeff looked back. "God, when this first happened I felt this hate, this anger—but Jesus," his words stopped—he was sobbing violently. It took a few minutes before he could speak again. "How could this happen? This wasn't Michele. Never. What happened?"

I felt like he really needed an answer. "I think Michele was suffering from severe postpartum depression."

"From what?"

"Postpartum depression."

"You mean this happens, other women have gone through this?"

I shook my head. "A fair number of women become seriously depressed, but it doesn't usually end in this sort of tragedy."

"I never heard of it," he said.

"Nobody really talks about it much. I've been thinking about that."

"So maybe this sort of caused Michele to act this way?"

"Maybe so."

He grew quiet, contemplative. I watched him thinking, unable to imagine sitting in his chair.

# 13

During those first excruciating weeks after Josh's birth, Jeff often spoke with his father. Glenn Remington tried to be supportive. He intended his offer of a place of live as an act of kindness.

"You know that place on Jefferson I own, the one next to your brother?"

"Yes," Jeff answered.

"Well, it's unoccupied at the moment, needs a little freshening, but you guys can have it rent-free while you're finishing your house."

As far as Jeff was concerned there was no decision. Their current place cost $500 a month, the neighbors seemed noisier than they had before there was a baby in the house, and Michele never did like the three flights of stairs. Jeff looked at his father and smiled. "That's great, I'll talk it over with Michele but I can't imagine she'll object." Father and son were both smiling as they shook hands. The deal was struck.

"Why not?" He was angry but he tried not to let it show.

Michele hesitated a moment before responding. She couldn't imagine how she could move. Something was wrong. She had no energy, every day was a struggle. She had to put up a front. She could hardly open a box of cereal or change Josh's diaper. The thought of packing, uprooting, moving, and unpacking— even if it was just a few blocks—was overwhelming. But more than that she couldn't stand the place.

Her mind again reran the tape of the house, which she had just visited earlier that day. She knew that Jeff looked at the tiny house and saw dollar signs—five hundred a month that would go toward building materials. What she saw was different.

One twelve Jefferson Avenue. An unoccupied ugly faded yellow dwarf with peeling brown trim standing so close to its neighbors on either side that sunlight seemed to be banned from the interior. The dark living room, the largest room, measured only twelve by fourteen feet. Two tiny bedrooms, a cramped kitchen, and a postage-stamp bath completed the picture. Furniture they had been accumulating for the new house was already crowding their current apartment, which was bigger than Jefferson Street. If they moved, it would be like living in a dark, dismal storage shed. Michele almost felt nauseous. I really can't do this, she thought. Something is wrong.

Her voice had no emotion when she spoke out loud. "Please, honey, moving would just be too much and I can't stand that place."

Jeff didn't understand. His annoyance with his wife had been growing and this was too much. It just didn't make sense. He felt the muscles of his jaw tighten but held his anger in check and spoke quietly. "Sorry, honey, this is something we've got to do."

The normal Michele, the feisty Michele, the Michele he had married would have laughed. "Maybe *you're* moving," she would have said. But this Michele just lowered her head.

"You won't have to lift a finger," was Jeff's final comment.

*   *   *

With the help of friends Jeff moved to 112 Jefferson on March 21. Michele was inefficiently present. As the crow flies this move was less than a mile in a southerly direction, but for Michele the direction was straight down.

# 14

The early morning sky was sunless with just a hint of transition from one cloud mass to the next. Jeff opened the kitchen door. March had come in like a lion and on this last day of the month it was still raw. A fine mist hung in the thirty-degree air and a light breeze added to the chill; not a pleasant day to be nailing shingles on someone's roof—but not bad enough to stay home. Jeff closed the door. The dishes from the previous evening's meal lay undisturbed in the sink. Joshua had been up at 3:00 A.M. and Jeff had given him his bottle; Michele was almost never able to awaken herself. When was she going to snap out of these doldrums?

As the water boiled, Jeff scooped a heaping mound of instant coffee into his mug and poured. Quickly he began to feel better. Grabbing a few outer layers—a sweater, shell, and an extra wool shirt—as well as his woolen mittens with the finger ends snipped off, he took one last peek at his son before leaving. Josh was sleeping soundly and looked content. Michele was still sleeping and he wouldn't disturb her.

The soft toot of the horn outside signaled the arrival of his ride. A little tired but looking forward to his day, Jeff picked his way through the furniture in the cluttered living room and at six-thirty stepped into the raw March morning.

\* \* \*

Two hours later Helen Cort drove up. The house looked dark, even beyond the hour and the bleakness of the day. She had a growing certainty that there was something seriously wrong with her daughter. Although Michele did protest weakly that she was "okay—just tired," mother knew better.

Helen walked to the front door and knocked firmly. No answer. She knocked again, and this time thought she heard a mumbled "come in." The knob turned easily. The living room, dark even on a sunny day, looked black on this gray morning. When her eyes began to adjust to the gloom she saw Michele sitting in the corner in a big overstuffed chair. Helen had the sense that she had been there for a while. Moving closer, she could tell her daughter had been crying.

"What's wrong?" she asked softly.

Michele began to rock slowly back and forth, the movement was small but somehow frightening. Helen asked more urgently, "What's wrong, honey?"

"I don't know, mom," Michele whispered.

Watching her daughter slowly rocking back and forth with tears silently crawling down her cheeks, Helen could stand no more. She had been even more upset than usual with her son-in-law. He should have been the one to get help. Now, Jeff or no Jeff, she would take matters into her own hands. With quick movements she silently began to straighten the clutter.

Michele watched her mother and knew. "What are you doing, mom?"

"Cleaning—this place is a mess."

"You have that look on your face."

"What look?"

Michele didn't answer.

"Look, honey, something is wrong. I'm going to call Dr. Murray. Someone needs to see you."

Michele just shrugged. She almost said, "It won't help," but she looked down at the floor instead. She had no interest in seeing Dr. Murray that day. He couldn't help; no one could. All week she had been thinking and had become convinced that she was worthless and her life was meaningless and everyone would be better off without her. She had thought so much about this that somehow she believed she had actually been discussing it with her family, but that was not the case. Her mother knew nothing of these thoughts, and nothing of the misty figure that had been part of Michele's existence. Any discussions that Michele remembered existed only in her delusional mind. Still, in that moment, although she did not understand why her mother would even bother, she did not have the strength to resist. If mom insisted that she go, Michele would see the doctor.

At 9:00 A.M. on the dot Helen picked up the phone and dialed, becoming impatient as the dial slowly spun back into place. She had Touch-Tone at home and it was much quicker. Dr. Murray's phone rang twice.

"Good morning, Dr. Murray's office." The voice was female.

"Good morning. This is Helen Cort, my daughter is Michele Remington—Dr. Murray delivered her baby a little more than a month ago."

"Yes, Mrs. Cort, what can I do for you?"

"Well—there's something terribly wrong with my daughter." Helen paused. "She seems totally withdrawn; for weeks she has hardly been able to care for herself or her son. It's getting worse and I know it's just not normal."

"Does she have any specific symptoms?" asked the voice.

"What do you mean?"

"Bleeding? Pain?"

"No, nothing like that—I can't tell you how totally out of it she seems, but it's bad."

"Depressed?"

"Yes, I think she's very depressed." Helen paused again and then said, "Look, I know Dr. Murray must be busy—but this is really important—I'm really worried about my daughter, maybe it is something physical, but I'm really worried about her."

There was a brief silence, then the voice said, "Mrs. Cort, can I put you on hold for a moment?"

"Okay."

In a minute the voice returned, "Mrs. Cort, Michele has her six-week appointment on Tuesday, that's just six days from now. Dr. Murray is totally booked today, and it looks as if he is going to have to cancel the morning as it is because of an emergency C-section. I know there's just no way he can see Michele today."

Helen was extremely upset. Michele, quietly listening to her mother's end of the conversation, watched her face grow red. Then her mother said "What is your name?"

"It's Virginia."

"Look, Virginia—this is serious, my daughter has been sitting, rocking, crying, and it's been going on for a long time. There must be a way Dr. Murray can see her—can I at least speak with him?"

It's not clear whether Kevin Murray was even in the office at that moment, but just as a football team tries to protect its quarterback, the overstressed doctor's staff often protects him, sometimes with his knowledge, sometimes without. As Virginia began to speak, Helen immediately sensed a change in attitude.

"Mrs. Cort—Dr. Murray will see Michele on the sixth. Don't worry—it's only the baby blues!"

"Look," Helen began, but before she was able to say more,

Virginia, whose voice was now as tough as any blocking fullback, cut in. "I'm sorry, Mrs. Cort, it's just not possible today."

"Thank you," Helen hissed as she slammed the phone into its cradle. Michele had to be seen. With great determination she picked up the phone again, but this time she dialed the number of Ben Greer, her own doctor.

# 15 ~

The office in Hoosick Falls, New York, seemed busy, but they did not have to wait long. Dr. Greer's nurse appeared at the door to the waiting room. "Mrs. Remington, Mrs. Cort, could you come this way please." Helen got up, carrying Joshua in her arms. Michele slowly followed her.

They were led into the doctor's office and offered chairs. Ben Greer joined them about two minutes later. The two women were silent. The baby was dozing. Michele was looking at the floor.

Slender and looking younger than his thirty-five years, Ben Greer's voice is surprisingly deep and resonant. "Good morning."

"Good morning," Helen replied, "thanks so much for seeing Michele." Michele said nothing, and Helen continued. "Michele didn't really want to come but I feel that something has to be done. For the past two weeks I don't know my daughter. She just sits—hardly says anything—hardly does anything around the house—and frankly," Helen paused, she was looking at Michele—this was hard to say in front of her daughter but she felt she had to convey the seriousness of the situation, "frankly—she doesn't seem that interested in the baby."

Ben Greer was watching Michele as her mother spoke. Still no eye contact, no change in expression. He looked back to Helen.

She compressed her lips, raised her eyebrows and made a slight gesture with her right hand and glanced from Michele back to Greer, as if to silently ask, "Now do you see what I mean?"

Greer's voice was quiet and warm. "Do you mind if I call you Michele?"

Michele's head remained bowed but she shook it "No."

"Michele, is your mom describing things pretty accurately?"

This time the small movements of Michele's head indicated yes.

"Do you understand why you've been this way?"

Michele was surprised, not by the question but by her feeling. Although she had never met Dr. Greer before, she instinctively liked him and for the first time in a while almost wanted to talk. She looked up and saw his eyes. "No, I don't really understand. I've just been so tired and I've had a stomach ache a lot of the time."

Greer nodded. For a few moments he was quiet and then he turned toward Helen. "Perhaps I could speak with Michele alone for a few minutes."

"Sure." Helen got up, taking Joshua in her arms. "Honey, please talk to Dr. Greer."

Michele made no movement whatsoever.

Ben Greer was silent for a few moments after Helen left. "Your mother can get pretty upset about things."

Michele looked up again, "Yeah, she can."

"But it does sound as though you've been pretty miserable."

All of a sudden Michele felt a tightness in her throat, so bad it almost hurt. Tears came to her eyes. "What is wrong with me?" she thought, trying not to sob. She could only nod.

Already Greer doubted whether a physical exam or a blood test would explain the "fatigue." He understood that she was depressed. He would do the exam but the real heart of this visit would be their discussion. He took a slightly different tack. "How's your appetite?"

"Bad. Either I'm just not interested in eating or my stomach is bothering me."

"Been losing weight?"

Michele shrugged. "I don't know," she said softly.

"How have you been sleeping?"

"Terrible."

"Has the baby been keeping you up a lot?"

"He's up a couple of times and I'm usually awake or I wake right up, but Jeff's the one who gets up and takes care of him most of the time."

"How come you don't get up?"

"I don't know," she almost whispered her answer, "Jeff probably doesn't even know that I'm awake."

"I remember your mom telling me that Joshua was pretty sick in the beginning. How's he been doing?"

"I guess he's okay. I mean he seems fine. I was scared at first, but he seems fine. We've been giving him medicine twice a day, but that's it."

"But it sounds like somehow you're not enjoying Joshua as much as you expected?"

Michele thought to herself, "He knows—he knows I'm not a good mother."

Ben Greer felt her withdrawal; he felt her sadness. "For some women it's very hard in the beginning. Your situation was very difficult—it's not unusual to be discouraged."

Michele nodded.

"So you have had little energy, have been having trouble sleeping, your appetite is down, and your stomach is bad, and it's hard to do things or even have an interest in things, and you've been feeling pretty bad about it all?"

Michele again nodded yes.

"I know we've never even met before and I'm sure it's not easy to talk right now, but I hope you don't mind. I'm really interested in helping."

"It's okay," Michele was surprised that she meant it.

"Michele, sometimes in situations like this someone can feel like giving up, like nothing is worth it. Have you felt that way?"

Michele nodded yes. Her eyes were again filled with tears.

"Have you had thoughts of suicide?" Greer's voice was soft.

"How does he know?" Michele thought. She looked at Ben Greer. There was something in his face, his eyes, that made it easy—"Yes," she answered softly.

Ben Greer knew what to ask next, a question crucial to deciding what must be done to help. He spoke almost casually. "Have you thought about how you would do it? In other words, do you have any plans for doing it?"

At the moment Ben Greer asked that question, Michele had her hand in her pocket. In her hand was a small bottle of over-the-counter sleeping pills that she was thinking about using to end it all. Should she tell him? Something made her want to. She looked again at Ben Greer—the signals from her motor cortex went racing along the neurons to the muscles of her mouth and vocal cords. Just before she spoke, in that microsecond, a buzzer went off and the voice of Dr. Greer's receptionist intruded through the speakerphone. "Dr. Greer, it's Dr. Schwartz on line one."

If at all possible Ben Greer took other physicians' calls as they came in. He picked up the phone. The conversation was brief, but within that time, for reasons she has never understood, Michele decided to say nothing about the pills. The nerve signals already sent by her brain were recalled.

"Thanks very much, John." She heard Dr. Greer end the conversation. It couldn't have been more than thirty seconds. Greer turned back to her.

"Sorry we were interrupted," he said, then continuing, "So do you have any plans?"

Michele just shook her head, "No." Her hand came out of her pocket; the pills remained hidden. Greer accepted the answer and felt a bit relieved.

At that point Dr. Greer was genuinely surprised by the question that popped into his head. He could not remember the last time he had even thought to ask such a question. "Michele, there are times when someone becomes so discouraged that they not only think about harming themselves, but they have thoughts about harming the baby as well. That can be very scary. Have any thoughts like that been troubling you?"

Michele felt like she had been slapped. "What must he think of me?" she thought. "I must seem crazy."

Out loud, she said, "No, I wouldn't do that."

Greer again sensed that she was shaken by the question, but every instinct led him to believe that she was telling the truth. I am convinced that his judgment at that moment was correct. Michele's thoughts were exclusively of harming herself.


During the brief and unremarkable physical exam that followed, Ben Greer was even more convinced that Michele was suffering from postpartum depression. He made a comment that some doctors have difficulty making, and so many patients have difficulty accepting. "Michele, you've been feeling so depressed, I think it might be a good idea for you to speak with a psychiatrist."

Ben Greer remembers that Michele declined. Edith Welton, Dr. Greer's nurse who was present while he examined her, also remembers that Michele declined. Michele does not remember the suggestion being made.

The exam completed, Greer returned to his office and dictated the following note while Michele dressed. Had Armageddon not been four days away, the note would seem relatively routine.

3/31/87

Postpartum Depression

*Subjective:* Patient was restricted for two months prior to her delivery for edema of her legs, and apparently had a double setup—

difficult forceps delivery, traumatized child who was transferred to Albany on the ventilator for ten days. Since then the child has been up a lot at night and they recently moved. She states she is very tired, she has diffuse abdominal pain which is not at all troubled by eating. She has been constipated, feels tired all the time, is not able to do things AND DOES HAVE SOME SUICIDAL THOUGHTS BUT NO PLANS. NO THOUGHTS OF HARMING THE CHILD.

*Objective:* Weight 163. BP 100/60. HEENT exam is unremarkable. Mucous membranes are moist. Neck is supple, lungs clear, cardiac exam shows regular rhythm without murmurs, rubs or gallop. Abdomen shows a very mild diffuse tenderness, without guarding, masses or rebound. Rectal was guaiac negative. THROUGHOUT THE EXAM THE PATIENT KEPT HER EYES ON THE FLOOR AND HAD POOR EYE CONTACT.

*Assessment:* I THINK SHE HAS SOMATIC SYMPTOMS IN RESPONSE TO HER MAIN PROBLEM WHICH IS DEPRESSION.

*Plan:* Colace. Follow up with me in one week. She is to call before then should she feel worse. Blood count and chemistry screen. CONTINGENCY FOR PSYCHIATRIC REFERRAL.

*Signed:* BEN GREER, M.D.


Dr. Greer returned to the exam room. Michele was ready and he accompanied her to the reception area where Helen and Joshua were waiting. Helen stood. Dr. Greer spoke first. "Helen, I think that Michele is very tired and depressed. She needs rest and supervision and help with the baby. Is there any way that someone might be with her during this next week?"

Helen contemplated the possibilities. Jeff knew nothing of this visit. As much as she had wanted to talk with him about Michele's situation, she found she just couldn't. It was ridiculous—two people who cared for Michele as much as any two people in the world, yet they were unable to work together in any way. She thought, "If I ask him to stop work for a week he would explode—especially if *I* ask him. Better if Michele stays with us, but I'd better have Philip talk with Jeff about this. Jeff will always be more reasonable with Philip."

"Michele and Josh can stay with her father and me," she said to Dr. Greer. "We will be happy to have them."

"Well, if that's okay with her husband it seems like a reasonable solution. Why don't you make an appointment for Michele to return to see me next week, and if she seems worse give me a call sooner."

"I will," Helen said, "and thanks very much." She extended her hand, which Ben Greer accepted. He then turned to Michele and extended his hand. "I hope you begin to feel better."

Michele nodded, took his hand, shook it briefly and quietly said, "Thanks."

Ben Greer did not really understand why he lingered in the waiting room to watch grandmother, mother, and baby leave his office.

# 16 🪶

Melanie, one of the clerks at the store, answered the phone. "Mr. Cort, it's for you—it's Mrs. Cort." Philip nodded and walked into his office. He picked up the extension. Melanie put her phone back into the cradle. Helen waited for the click.

"Honey, there's something definitely wrong with Michele. I've just taken her to see Dr. Greer and he thinks she's very depressed. He suggested that someone should be with her this week and that she should get plenty of rest."

"What can we do?"

"I don't think Jeff would react kindly to a suggestion that he stay home with her all week—so I want Michele and the baby to stay with us for a little while, but I don't want to talk to Jeff alone."

On the other end of the line Philip closed his eyes briefly, compressed his lips, shook his head and sighed—none of which his wife was aware of. When Helen pushed, she pushed. "What does Michele think?"

"She doesn't seem to care very much about anything one way or the other. If we all agree, she'll go along with it."

"Helen, I'm not too sure about this." He paused, but there was no response, and he sighed again. "Okay, I'll meet you at their place after work, say about seven."

"Thanks."

Helen walked from the kitchen to the living room and glanced at Michele. She somehow sensed that Michele had overheard the conversation.

"You heard what I said to dad?"

Michele nodded almost imperceptibly. There was no further discussion. Helen straightened a few things, kissed her daughter on the forehead, and said, "We'll see you later, honey. Will you be okay?"

Michele nodded again.

The little house seemed especially dark and quiet after Helen left. Slowly rocking back and forth, her son napping in his crib, Michele could envision the scene that lay ahead. Jeff would be tired and exasperated; dad, quiet and nervous; mom, upset and insistent. And she would be just a leaf in a breeze, without attachment, moving in whatever direction the others wanted.

At that moment Michele felt not the slightest hope that she would ever improve. No one could help. "You are a failure Michele—you're a failure." There was that voice. She put her hands over her ears as if it would shut out the thoughts.

Rocking. So tired. Unable to focus, to concentrate, sometimes unable to remember what she had done just a few moments before. Worthless. Guilty for not being able to care—to feel for her son whose arrival had been so joyfully anticipated. Michele hated herself. She had to die.

Three times in the past two weeks she had decided there was no alternative but to end her life. Three times she had changed her mind. This was the fourth decision and somehow it felt more real. She would find the right moment, either at home or at her parents', and she would take the pills that she had not shown to Dr. Greer.

It may have been ten minutes or it may have been two hours after her mother left. Michele stood up and walked to the small desk in the corner of the living room. There she wrote a letter to her husband.

*My Jeffrey,*

*God, how can I ever expect you to understand or live with what I've done. I'm so sick of not feeling good and not being able to take care of everyday things, you and our baby. I keep trying to overcome this thing, but it won't go away. There's something terribly wrong with me physically and emotionally. I can't eat or sleep, my arms and legs are so weak and my stomach feels like it's been cut out. I haven't been able to go to the bathroom normally in two weeks, I feel like I'm in knots and every time Josh breast-feeds he gets whatever I have.*

*I keep pushing to function every day because it hurts me to see you worried to a frazzle trying to help me and going to work too. Before long you'll end up sick. I'm so tired of having to depend on people who have lives of their own, my poor mother has done everything for me when she needs so desperately to take care of herself.*

*I shouldn't have gotten pregnant. My body has not been right and when Josh was born it took everything I had and I can't get it back. After all the planning and the anticipation of his coming, I couldn't even do that right. I gave you a son who wasn't just the way it was supposed to be, and now there're all these things we have to worry about, praying he'll be healthy and normal, but never really knowing for sure for months and months to come.*

*Emotionally I guess I can't handle it. I feel guilty. Somehow I'm being punished because this is all my fault. The only thing I wanted was to have children with you but now I'm too scared to even think about being pregnant again after what I've put you through and what happened to him. How could I ever have another and go through all the motions with another child when I can't even take care of one now? I guess you could call me an unfit mother. Somebody's trying to tell me I'm not cut out for this. I can't even do my own housework or make you nice dinners.*

*All the things I dreamed of with you are shattered and I'm just dragging you down with me. You have such a terrific outlook on things and so much stamina, I wish I was like you. I never have really liked myself, it seems I've always sort of limped through life on one leg. I could never figure out what my purpose was for being here except I kind of thought it was to have beautiful, well-behaved, normal children, but I couldn't even do that right. Everything I've always done hasn't been normal. Every time I've been sick it hasn't been normal, and then I seem to do stupid things like moving up to a third floor twice.*

*The only thing that ever mattered was loving you. I can't drag you down any more. You deserve so much better than me and financially I'm going to take you down because I can't even think about going to work because of the way I feel and trying to take on everyday things too. I can't do it. I'd lose my job and then everything will be in the hole.*

*I won't be a total burden. I was used to being independent and taking care of things myself. I know it will be hard for a while, but you're stronger than I am and you will do what has to be done, you told me that just a few days ago. At least you'll rest now and I can sleep too, that's all I've thought about for the past couple of days, going to sleep and never waking up and I won't have to fight to eat, my appetite has been zilch lately and the only way to get strong is to eat and nothing appeals to me and I have to shove stuff down my throat. I can't stand it.*

> *All I want to do is sleep.*
>
> *I love you always,*
>
> MICHELE

Michele put down her pen; she almost felt relief. Scanning the room she noticed the bills stacked on a table near the door to the kitchen. Jeff hated the bills. It was strange but she smiled for the first time in a week. She walked to the table and slipped the letter to the bottom of the pile. There it would be safe. Jeff would have to look at the bills eventually, but by then it would be over.

# 17 🍂

It was about seven-fifteen when Jeff opened the front door. Michele watched his smile disappear as he saw her parents in the living room. Helen was actually quivering. She looked as though she was about to jump out of her skin. Philip looked pale and uncomfortable, but it was he who began the conversation.

"How've you been, Jeff?"

Jeff moved closer and shook his father-in-law's hand. "Okay—how about you?"

"Fine, thanks."

Helen remained silent and Jeff did not acknowledge her. After a brief but tense pause, Phil continued. "Michele went to Dr. Greer today and he thinks she's very depressed and that's causing most of her problems. This happens sometimes to new mothers—and—well—he feels she needs complete rest and so we thought that maybe she and Josh should stay with us for a few days." He glanced down. It was hard to look his son-in-law in the eye.

Jeff didn't miss a beat. "No way. If Michele wants to go that's up to her but Joshua stays here."

No one said anything. No one pointed out that if Jeff were going to be home all the time Michele could stay. There was just silence. If Michele was a silent leaf drifting in the wind, Jeff was a silent chunk of burning coal going from red- to white-hot.

Helen was a nerve ending, afraid to say anything. Philip was just silent.

There were few words after that. Jeff walked to the bedroom, found the small suitcase, grabbed a few handfuls of Michele's clothes from the bureau, stuffed them hard into the suitcase, came back to the room, and silently handed it to Philip.

*I was just like a big puppet. Everyone else pulled the strings and I just danced. It seemed as though I had no will at all. I think I said "I'm sorry, honey" as we left—I don't think Jeff said goodbye.*

*A half-hour later I was sitting alone in my old bedroom feeling more guilty and worthless than ever. My parents live in Arlington, a few minutes north of Bennington. Their home is surrounded by woods and I used to love the quiet beauty, the play of light and shadow. There was a moon that night and through all my pain the view from my childhood window still calmed me a little.*

*I had been sitting only a few minutes when my mom called upstairs and asked me to come down to eat. I wasn't really hungry but I went anyway. I sat with my parents at the table, silent and unhappy. Mom was beside herself. She didn't know what to do. "Please, Michele," she said, "you've got to eat, you've got to snap out of this—you have a wonderful little boy." Then she started on Jeff. "He should have taken better care of you, he should have taken you to the doctor," and on and on. I said nothing. I figured she was trying to get me stirred up, to get me upset or excited or something, but nothing worked.*

*The more she spoke, however, the more I knew she was right. I was nothing—just absolutely no good. I couldn't really understand why they wanted me around. Finally they left the table and I was alone.*

*Everything seemed wrong as I looked around the house of*

*my youth. It seemed empty. My parents' lives seemed empty. I remember thinking that I didn't want to be like them. Nothing seemed to matter.*

*I don't actually remember getting up and going to my bedroom, but I did and sometime in the midst of that morbid, bleak, hopeless evening, I fell asleep.*

*When I awakened the next morning I felt terrible, the kind of terrible inside that's almost a physical pain but it's not. Nothing had changed.*

*I was so tired, even though I couldn't remember being up it felt as though I hadn't slept. The house was quiet—so quiet I thought it must be very early but my watch said it was eight-forty-five. April Fools' Day.*

*At first I thought, "Dad must have gone to work and mom must be out doing errands." Then it struck me, knowing my mother I was surprised that she would have left me alone—sleeping.*

*I got out of bed and walked to the window. I could see the front path. Mom was standing there with Eva, one of her best friends. Mom was crying and Eva had her arm around her shoulder. "Look what I'm doing," I thought, "this can't go on." At that moment I decided—today was the day.*

*On my desk were a few sheets of plain white paper and a few pencils. I sat down and wrote a note to my parents— explaining. I really remember little about the rest of that day, except that I was obsessed with the thought of taking those sleeping pills.*

*Finally it was time. I thought my parents would stop me from going upstairs because I felt as though I had slipped and was saying goodbye. I must not have used that word, however, because they didn't act as though anything was wrong.*

*I walked upstairs in a peculiarly calm frame of mind. I*

*was feeling more at peace than I had for days. I went into the bathroom and looked at the pills. I'm sure there was a label with the name of the medication, but I have no idea what that label said. I don't know how many there were, but it took a while to get the pills down. As I was swallowing the last one I had a fleeting feeling of disbelief that I was actually doing this, then a few moments of regret, then just a sense of quiet. I was convinced that everyone— especially Jeff and Joshua—would be better off without me. When I turned out the light in the bathroom, I honestly believed that I would never awaken again.*

*I slipped between the covers of my childhood bed knowing that it would be my final resting place. I was genuinely sad that this was my parents' home and sorry for the extra pain that would cause, but I was too tired to fight. I just wanted to sleep forever.*

*I was suddenly awake and after a few moments remembered what I had done. Maybe this was the beyond? I struggled to understand. I had spent years of nights in that room and knew it well. Directly opposite my bed was the large window from which I had seen my mother crying the morning before. I was aware that it was not completely dark outside, but I seemed to be having trouble seeing. The windows seemed tiny and very far away. As much as I tried, I could not bring it into focus. I became frightened. "Oh, God," I thought, "I'm going to live through this and I'm going to have brain damage."*

*I thought I yelled out loud, but if I did it couldn't have been loud because my parents' room was nearby and they would have awakened. You can hear everything in that house. Then I must have passed out again.*

# 18 🪶

Joshua had been up once during the night. Other than that father and son slept peacefully. At the late hour of nine-thirty Jeff awakened feeling very refreshed. Perhaps the novelty would wear off, but he had really enjoyed the day he spent with his son and looked forward to their second day together. He missed Michele but he didn't miss her constant gloom and irritability and he was angry that she had simply given in to her mother's pressure and left home.

After a fresh cup of coffee and a few minutes with the Bennington *Banner*, he went to check Josh, who was still sleeping soundly. Soon, however, his morning medicine was due and Jeff could not remember what he had done with it. Walking back to the living room, his eyes searched for the bottle. The desk was especially cluttered; perhaps it was hidden amongst the junk. A shirt that he had been wearing the night before lay on top of the clutter. Moving it, he dislodged a few of the bills that had been sitting on the top of the piles. They fluttered to the floor. Reaching down he picked them up and put them back on the desk. As he did, he noticed a few yellow sheets of paper on the bottom of the pile that had some writing.

For a moment Jeff forgot his search for the medicine. Extracting the sheets he began to read. His stomach began to churn. Halfway through the letter he turned without looking up and walked toward the phone in the kitchen, still reading.

The thought did cross Helen's mind that it was unusual for Michele to be sleeping until almost ten in the morning, but she felt she was just "catching up." Busying herself in the kitchen, glad that her daughter was finally getting some rest, she just put the last dish into the drainer on the sink when the phone rang. It was her son-in-law and as usual he didn't address her directly. She was neither Helen nor mom.

"Where's Michele?" Jeff asked.

"She's asleep."

"Wake her—I just found a letter she must have written before she went to your house and I think she might try to hurt herself. I think she might have taken some sleeping pills."

Helen could not believe what Jeff was saying. She didn't want to believe that this could actually happen. "Don't be silly," she blurted, "we don't have anything like that in the house."

Jeff's anger fired through the telephone. "Damn it, Helen, would you go and check on her."

Helen put the phone down, shaken. She walked up the stairs and opened the door to Michele's room. Michele must have been in a semiconscious state. She remembers that the door opened—that she was somehow aware that her mother was looking in. Perhaps she stirred, because Helen closed the door and left. Had she walked into the room and tried to rouse Michele she might have known that something was wrong. She probably would also have seen the note lying on the bedside table. But she had been caught by a mixture of fear and denial. Michele was sleeping peacefully and had even moved. She closed the door and returned to the phone in the kitchen.

Helen reported her findings to Jeff. He was relieved but not convinced. Under normal circumstances, when he and Helen were at least being civil to one another, he would have probably gotten into the car and driven over. But not now. He hung up the phone, his stomach still in a knot.

Michele awakened about fifteen minutes later. Helen heard her get up and go into the bathroom. Jeff called again at that moment, determined that if Michele was still sleeping he would immediately drive to Arlington, Helen or no Helen. Told that Michele was out of bed he was relieved. "When she comes downstairs, have her call me," he demanded and the conversation ended.

While Jeff and her mother were on the phone, Michele tore up the note she had written to her parents.

# 19 🪶

Thursday, April 2, was a sunny day. The temperature hooked its finger over the fifty-degree mark in the early afternoon and hung on for a few hours. Michele awakened shortly after ten, feeling even more like a failure because she was still alive. But she could see and hear, and when she tested her voice she could speak. Apparently she would not be a vegetable.

After a brief stop in the bathroom she navigated the stairs. Her mother was in the kitchen and greeted her daughter with a smile. "Well, you must have really needed your sleep. Feel any better?"

"A little."

"How about a cup of coffee?"

"Sure."

While the water boiled Helen mentioned that Jeff had been calling. She said nothing of his suspicions. Michele immediately picked up the phone.

"Are you okay?" he asked.

"Yeah," was all Michele said at first. Then she continued. "Are you going to be around for a while?"

"Sure."

"Well, I think I'll take a ride and stop by later—if mom will let me have the car."

"Sounds good to me," Jeff said, and the moment for asking

Michele about her letter seemed to vanish. Perhaps he would ask her when she came over. Perhaps he could persuade her to stay.

*I don't know why I was going home. I don't know what I told Jeff, but I thought, "Well, maybe if I go back and I walk through the door I'll feel different. After being away for a couple of days maybe things will feel better. Maybe there will be something that will make me want to try again."*

*Mom didn't seem to suspect that my long sleep had been anything but exhaustion. She probably wanted to believe that a good sleep was all I needed, and she must have felt I was okay or she would never have let me borrow her car for the afternoon.*

*The few minutes of driving were pleasant. There was still no fresh green on the mountains, but the sun was shining and the chill that is always in the Vermont air during winter was gone. I prayed I would magically feel better, but as soon as I walked through the door I knew I wouldn't. In fact, I felt worse. After being in my parents' home the house on Jefferson Street seemed even smaller, and darker, and more cluttered than ever. And despite the hint of spring outside, inside that little house the winter chill remained.*

*The worst parts of those Thursday afternoon moments were my feelings about Josh. As soon as I walked through the door I realized that I couldn't care for him—that I didn't really want to be with him. I remember thinking, "How can I tell this to anyone? Nobody's going to accept this. They'd be horrified and just grab hold of me and say 'How can you think that—just snap out of it!'"*

*I didn't want to hurt him or anything; I just didn't want him, couldn't be with him. I didn't know what to do, but I couldn't stay there and I didn't want to go back to my* parents'. I thought of going to see my close friend Barbara. Throughout all of this she was always the one person who seemed to come closest to understanding me. Perhaps if I had gone to her I would have told her what was going on— I wish I had.

So there I was, even more certain than ever that I deserved to die. At that moment I didn't care about anything. I didn't care about Jeff, I didn't even care about my baby. Jeff was strong. He could take care of himself and Josh; he had already proven that. I figured it was no big loss if I wasn't around. This time I would take no chances, no more pills for me.

Since we had just moved I decided I had to check and make sure I could locate the gun that I learned to shoot when we managed the motel. As I went upstairs, Jeff asked me what I was doing. "Just getting a change of clothes."

I found the gun where I expected, on a closet shelf under a pile of sweaters. But the bullets were not there. I couldn't find them at first and became fearful that Jeff would be suspicious if I took too long. After what seemed like an eternity (but was probably five minutes), I found them in a shoe box on the floor of the same closet. I was relieved.

I was too afraid of being caught to try and take the gun and bullets back to my parents'. No, I would have to return to Jefferson Street. I changed my shirt but totally forgot that my excuse for coming upstairs had been my need for a change of clothes. When I came down empty-handed, Jeff noticed immediately.

"I thought you needed some clothes?"

I said nothing.

"What were you doing up there?"

Again I said nothing. I just didn't want to talk to him, and he was becoming upset. I had to get out.

*Jeff kept talking. "Don't let this thing go on too long, Michele, I want you to come home. You don't belong at your mother's, you belong here."*

I told him I had to return the car and he realized that was true. He could have offered to follow me but he didn't. *"I'll probably just stay there tonight, I'm just so tired—then I'll see how I feel in the morning."*

Jeff sort of threw up his hands. He wasn't at all happy, but he knows I'm stubborn and he knew that I wasn't going to change my mind.

I don't remember driving back. I don't remember coming into the house. My mother must have been there because I had her car, but I don't remember talking with her. I do remember sitting on the couch in the family room in the basement. It was in the late afternoon and the TV was on but I was paying no attention. It was just noise. Suddenly I felt a chill, someone else or something else was there with me.

The voice in my head was back, hounding me. It would come and go. It was saying, *"You are worthless, everyone would be better off without you."* Sometimes it seemed to be Jeff's voice, sometimes my mom's. Sometimes I would try to tell this voice that I was needed, that I was really a good person, that I would get over this. But the voice would continue longer than I could fight. I was being worn down, and after returning from Jefferson Street on that Thursday afternoon feeling that I had nowhere in the world to go, feeling totally beaten, the voice became my voice. Then it seemed to be coming from that body that was there with me. Perhaps this misty figure in the room was just another part of me. Everybody has a positive and a negative side and I thought maybe this was my negative side.

Then I noticed that my vision wasn't right. Normally I have pretty good peripheral vision and I can see people coming up beside me when they reach my shoulder. But that day I could only see what was directly in front of me. It was like being in a tunnel and everything off to the side was vague, fuzzy, and unclear. And that's just where this other whatever was sitting, off to the side. As always it was just a shape, a mist with no detail. There were the arms and hands with no fingernails. There was the head with no face, but now there was my voice.

Somehow this force, this creature, was drawing on my strength. The more I fought, the stronger it got. It was unbearable. If for a moment I tried to feel hopeful, it shot me down.

All week everything had been wrong. I was suspicious that my mother was constantly talking about me when she was on the phone. (This was probably true.) Whenever she tried to encourage me to eat, sleep, or become more interested in Josh or my home, I was unable to accept her words. Now I realize that everything she was saying made absolute sense, but then I just felt blamed and guilty that she was upset and I was the cause.

So as I sat there that Thursday afternoon trying to fend off this misty force, I was absolutely beaten. There was no fight left and no way out. I was certain. I had to go back to Jefferson Street, get Jeff out of the house, and load that gun.

I thought I knew where my heart was.

# 20 🍂

From the moment I opened my eyes on Friday morning I was "better." It was a miracle. I got up and went into the kitchen. My mother was already there. I opened the refrigerator door, then the pantry.

"What are you doing?" she asked.

"I'm hungry, I want something to eat."

For a moment mom seemed shocked. It was the first time in weeks that I had expressed any interest in food. Finally she said, "Just tell me what you want, honey, and I'll make it."

I don't remember what I ate but I do remember that mom and I seemed to really talk for the first time in a long while. Finally she said, "You seem more like your old self, like you're feeling a little better."

"Yeah, I guess so. I sort of feel like I've snapped out of it—almost like a rubber band. I'm not really sure why."

"That's wonderful, Michele. I hope things can get back to normal and you can begin to enjoy Joshua."

I hoped for the same thing. In fact, I was already thinking about Joshua. After all, I was the one who most wanted

a baby and now I was beginning to remember those feelings
for the first time. I wanted to be with him.

Despite the fact that this was so sudden, so unexplained,
mom didn't question the change. She was much too
grateful and I was genuinely sincere. I remember hugging
her and apologizing. I don't remember exactly what I
said, but I tried to make it right between us. When I said,
"I'm going home, mom, give me a few minutes to pack,"
she didn't protest. About forty-five minutes later she dropped
me off on Jefferson. Jeff must have heard the car because
the front door opened.

I remember the look on his face as I walked toward him.
I wasn't sure what his reaction was going to be, but he
seemed very happy—not at all upset at first. Then within a
few minutes I could see he was becoming edgy. I said
something like, "What is it?" He needed no further prodding.
He walked to the desk where I had left the letter three
days earlier. It was now plainly visible on top of the bills,
but until that moment I hadn't noticed it. Jeff picked it
up and asked what I was thinking when I wrote it. I was
surprised by the look on his face. I have never seen Jeff
cry, but for a brief moment he seemed to choke up.

If I didn't tell him what he already knew deep down, he
wouldn't have believed me. So I looked him in the eye
and said, "I was thinking about killing myself, but I don't
feel that way now and I'm not going to do anything like
that, so you can tear up that letter." I said nothing about
the pills that I had taken. He said nothing about the
multiple phone calls he had made to my mother just the day
before. He just looked at me, said, "Okay," and came
over and gave me a hug.

We were both happy not to have to talk about it any more.
Even mentioning the letter had been a bit of a downer, but

*I still felt good, better than I had in a long time. Not exactly my old self, but better. I began to straighten the apartment and remember thinking, "This place really is as terrible as I thought." Still, I did my best to organize the clutter.*

*After things were reasonably neat I headed for the desk. I was the one who usually looked after our finances, and during the few days I was away (except for that minute when he discovered my letter), Jeff had paid no attention to the bills that were sitting there. I discovered that in addition to those I had left, a few new ones had arrived. I sat down and figured out where we stood.*

*All in all, the day was routine, except that "routine" was so different from what my life had been that I almost felt high. Somehow, however, with all my activity, I still paid little attention to Joshua. I don't think that was as much disinterest as it was insecurity. It almost felt like my first day with him, and Jeff had become so proficient that I think I felt comfortable just letting him continue taking care of Josh. As the day went on I did a little more, but I was happy just to ease into motherhood gradually. Even that night Jeff continued to take the lion's share of the responsibility.*

*The only way one of us could really sleep in that tiny apartment was for that person to stay upstairs while the other person remained downstairs with Josh. It just worked out better. So that first night Jeff suggested that I get some sleep. He would stay downstairs. I kissed him goodnight, kissed Josh goodnight and went upstairs.*

Depressions end in different ways.

Sometimes happiness just sneaks up, a little at a time. Gradually, each day becomes easier and richer, until mood and life are back to normal.

Sometimes the departure is abrupt. The transformation from fatigue to energy, from apathy to motivation, from indecision to decisiveness, from confusion to clarity, from sadness to happiness, from gray to color, from darkness to light, can be so quick that it seems as though a curtain has suddenly lifted. Bang, you're better.

Unfortunately, when that happens the curtain does not always stay up. Before the recovery is solid there may be a number of curtain calls. First there is one very good day, then a few bad; then two good days and a few more bad. Finally the bad don't return and life begins anew.

Sometimes, after that first tease of good feeling, if the curtain does drop again the landscape may seem even more bleak, more hopeless, more "I'll really never get over this" than it did before. A gnawing sense of futility engulfs you. It's like that extra blackness of the bedroom after a middle-of-the-night trip to a lighted bathroom. For someone recovering from depression those moments of super darkness can be especially disheartening, frightening, and dangerous.

Almost as soon as Michele was alone in the darkness of her bedroom on Jefferson Street her fragile connection with her old self began to fail. Through the night there were only snatches of real sleep. In between these brief moments of relief were many agonizing glances at the clock, as though the power of vision could accelerate the luminous hands around the dial and make morning come sooner.

As it always does, even after the longest of nights, dawn arrived. Michele was wound up tighter than a watch spring but she did not stir. There was nowhere in that small house where she could go and not disturb Jeff and probably Josh as well. She did not want Jeff to awaken and ask questions—"What's wrong? Why can't you sleep? What was on your mind when you wrote that

81

letter? Are you feeling bad again?" If she had to open up to Jeff at that moment, the dam would burst. The good feelings of Friday would be washed away. She knew it. No—she would stay in bed until morning.

Lying on her right side, she reached up with her left hand and grabbed the edge of the headboard, clinging with the grip of a rock climber who had found the seam in the face of the cliff.


If Mother Nature had been kinder on April 4, perhaps Michele would have been able to maintain her desperate grip throughout the day, but Mother Nature was in a foul mood.

It was one of those days that stays dark. Winter does not leave Vermont gracefully. Almost every year, the first week in April brings one last snow. In 1987, on that Saturday, winter lost. It was almost cold enough to snow, but not quite. Snow is a much happier form of precipitation than rain. Ask anyone who lives in New England.

# 21 🪶

It wasn't until Jeff heard the rain that he realized he was awake. Pit, Pat, Tap, Tap, Tap on the window—then the drops became indistinguishable, striking too fast to be counted. Usually a heavy sleeper, it was surprising how easily he began to tune into night sounds when there was no one else around to hear Joshua's cries. He had been asleep less than two hours since Josh's last feeding and it took a few seconds to refocus. "Jefferson Street. Saturday morning. Michele is home."

Through the window the sky was beginning to lighten. Josh slept peacefully and there was no sound from the bedroom upstairs to indicate that his wife was awake. As he lay there listening to the music of the rain, his plans and dreams again seemed realistic. Michele would be her old self again. Once she was back to work there would be no difficulty in obtaining a construction loan to complete their house. By late summer or early fall they would move in—mom, dad, and Joshua. For the first time in days his morning face had a hint of a smile.

He thought briefly about going to Carpenter Hill to work on the house, but decided against it. Between the weather and the fact that it was Michele's first full day back, he wanted to remain close. Still, after four continuous days with Joshua, Jeff needed to be out.

In the yard behind the Jefferson Street house was a small red barn that his dad used for storage. One corner of the building had settled and the foundation was cracked. Jeff had noticed deterioration of some of the lower boards on that corner; the defect was like a slow cancer. The boards could easily have been replaced, but the wound would recur until major foundation surgery was performed. Glenn Remington had given the young couple the use of the Jefferson Street property until their new house was finished. Jeff was now only too happy to return the favor. He would "operate" and fix the foundation. Saturday would be spent jacking up the barn. The rain really didn't matter. With these thoughts in mind he pulled back the covers and arose from the bed to begin the day.

It started out innocently enough, a fresh pot of coffee, a little straightening, the usual morning scan of the Bennington *Banner*. Michele came down shortly after eight and they exchanged small talk. She seemed okay. She did not protest in the slightest when he told her of his plans to work in the back yard. He did not rush. It was about ten o'clock before he walked into the dark, wet, forty-four-degree morning.

When Michele called him for lunch two hours later he was surprised; he had no idea that much time had gone by. Thoroughly drenched, with wet tools, wet wood, a jammed jack, and more splitting siding, he was happy. The job would have been much easier with a fellow worker, but in the wetness and the solitude there was peace; his son's medical troubles and his wife's depression could almost be forgotten. Over the past week he had been under more stress than he realized, and this day of daydreams and hard work was cathartic.

After toweling off and changing to dry clothes Jeff sat down at the kitchen table. Michele put a bowl of chicken noodle soup and a ham and cheese sandwich in front of him—all of which he happily devoured. This was the way it was supposed to be, the family together, Michele caring for Josh. With the exception of her premenstrual moodiness Jeff had not often seen his wife depressed. He had no difficulty accepting this sudden return of her good sense and hopefulness and interest in their son. Sitting at the kitchen table, dry and fed, he was not overly concerned that Michele was quiet or that she didn't eat very much; that was not so unusual.

The rain continued to pour from the sky in sheets. Within fifteen minutes Jeff finished the meal and returned to his work, wet and happy again.


Twice during the afternoon Jeff came in briefly for a cup of hot coffee. For the first time in a while Michele seemed settled. He did notice that Barbara Loggia had come to visit, but he had not been inside while she was there. He was trying to get as much done as possible.

The afternoon wore on and slowly lost its grip to the advance of evening. This was the last day of Standard Time—that night the clocks would be moved forward one hour and Daylight Saving Time would begin. Jeff wished the time change had already taken place. By five-thirty on this dark and dreary day it was difficult to continue working. Lights were blinking on in the homes up and down the street. His own house, however, remained dark. Jeff hadn't noticed.

# 22

My first day home and I already wanted to leave. The plan was to spend the day at Barbara Loggia's. Of all my friends she was the most tuned in to how I felt. Josh and I could go over to her house and she would take care of both of us. We would be okay, and Jeff could have his much deserved day off. Then I became aware of the weather.

The rain was pounding on the roof. I got out of bed and went downstairs. The living room, which was normally dark, was especially gloomy, and it didn't occur to me to turn on the lights.

Jeff mentioned that he thought Josh was getting a cold, and I knew it would be irresponsible of me to take him out in this weather. I just couldn't ask Jeff to stay with Josh again while I took off to visit my friend. Besides, if I had asked him to do that, he would have probably gotten annoyed, probably asked questions, and I felt that I couldn't deal with anything.

I'm not sure exactly what I did to pass the time. When the hour was decent I remember calling Barbara. Perhaps she could come to visit since I couldn't go to visit her.

I remember sitting on the sofa and feeling wet. It was strange. I actually felt as though the rain was falling inside the room. I began to obsess about the wetness. It seems unbelievable to me now, but at one point I may have taken an umbrella and held it over Josh's crib. I also have a memory, or perhaps more a feeling, that I took off my clothes and stood in the middle of the living room trying to dry off with one of those huge beach towels. I thought that Jeff came in and I had to explain to him why I was doing these things, only he says he never saw any of this, and I guess he's right because I'm sure if he had he would have carted me off to the hospital.

It's difficult now to convey the confusion of that morning. Maybe I did those things, maybe not. Perhaps Jeff just didn't come in at the right time. I suspect, however, that it was all in my mind. I wish to God I had acted crazy.

It was probably in the mid-morning when he returned— that misty faceless figure who haunted me at my parents' house. I didn't want him to be there again, but he was. First a glimpse out of the corner of my eye—then the voice. I don't remember the words, but they tore away the thin covering of good feeling that was left over from Friday afternoon. At that moment, I knew with certainty what I had known for weeks. I was bad—a bad mother, a bad wife, a bad person. I remember feeling as alone as I have ever been. I wanted to give up. Time became meaningless. I was just sitting in a damp grayness in my own personal fog.

There must have been some fight left in me because I struggled. I don't know how to put this but I was trying to keep me intact. I sat immobile, doing nothing, but that required all of my strength.

If Joshua had made any demands on me that morning, I'm not sure what I would have done, but he was very quiet. Actually too quiet. Despite my relief that he was not fussy,

*I remember moments that morning when his lethargy
upset me. My older brother Michael had been given
phenobarbital, and it completely tamed him. Josh was
being given the same medication, and he was sleeping
constantly. I know it makes no sense because I didn't
think I could deal with any normally active child, but I was
feeling cheated.*

*There had been times in the weeks before April 4 when I
did things just to awaken my son. Sometimes I ran the
vacuum cleaner, sometimes played loud music, even shook
him gently on occasion. If he did stir, he would quickly
fall back to sleep. I felt that I hadn't really met my son,
didn't really know him. There were moments I was so
frustrated and so worried I would just cry.*

*It was about one o'clock when Jeff came in for lunch. I
managed to make him a sandwich and a bowl of soup.
He was drenched but it didn't seem to bother him. I just
couldn't understand that at all. He ate quickly and we
spoke very little. In a few minutes he disappeared again into
the rain. I said nothing about my anguish, my
hopelessness, or my misty visitor who always left when
someone else was around. I made a sandwich for myself.
It lay on the plate hardly touched.*

*Suddenly I couldn't stand being alone. Earlier I had phoned
Barbara to tell her that I was not able to visit. She had
been planning to come over later in the afternoon. I called
again at that point—"Could you come sooner?" In about
half an hour I heard her knock on the door.*

*I was relieved to see her but she totally depressed me
because she looked so terrific and I just couldn't pull
myself together. No matter what I did or how hard I tried,
I felt inadequate.*

*Barbara had an umbrella that she shook out and placed*

in the corner of the room. After removing her raincoat
she sat down quietly on the sofa. Trying not to awaken Josh
she spoke in a very soft voice and asked me how I was
doing. I really don't remember any specific details of that
conversation, but she must have had some sense that not
all was well.

As if he somehow knew that someone was around who
could really take care of him, within ten minutes of
Barbara's arrival, Josh awakened.

She asked me if she could hold him and I said, "Sure." It
hurt to see how easily he was comforted by her. Often,
when I would pick him up he would continue to cry. I was
actually jealous.

I grew even more upset as I watched Barbara change him.
It was clear to me how good she was and how inept I
was. It was then that the thought occurred to me, "Barbara
should take Josh home with her." It was just a vague
thought, there was no special length of time in mind, maybe
it would be just for the day, but something was telling
me he would be better off.

It was as though Barbara had read my mind. I got goose
bumps when I heard her say, "He's just so cute, Michele,
I would love to borrow him for a while."

"Would you?" I asked. "That would be okay." I meant it.

Barbara looked up with a strange expression on her face,
then she chuckled and gave me a second look, but that
was it. She just sat there making my son contented. Maybe
I should have been more insistent that she take Josh. In
some ways, when I remember that conversation, I feel as
though I was insistent, but it must not have been the
case.

Barbara stayed for almost an hour and I did feel a little
better. Finally, at about three-thirty she said, "I still have
a few errands to do and I have to go." I didn't want her to

*leave but I had no choice. As soon as the door closed, I
felt dreadfully alone again. I remember thinking, "I've got
to get out of this and start acting right. Jeff will be in for
dinner soon and I should try to get something together."*

*I went to the kitchen but somehow I couldn't even begin
to organize a simple meal. Then, suddenly, the room
seemed filled with different voices and different faces. It was
almost like being in an echo chamber, the volume swelling and
receding like the ocean.*

*I ran back into the living room and took some pillows and
put them over my ears but there was no relief. The words
followed me, demanding and directing, "Get the gun and do
it!" The voices were like a force urging me to kill myself.
It seemed as though they were correct. It was the only
solution. I was totally lost and unhappy. I remember
nothing further. Nothing at all until I heard Jeff come into
the house. By then it was too late.*

Barbara Loggia hadn't been in the office for more than thirty
seconds and she was already choking back tears. Dark, attractive,
Italian, mid-thirties, and very feeling, I liked her immediately.

"I hope you didn't mind me calling." She seemed very nervous.

"Not at all—actually Michele suggested that I talk with you."

"This has been so horrible for me, but that's not why I'm here.
I don't know if you are aware of this but Michele will only go
out to come to your office or my house. Nowhere else. We've
had a chance to talk a little and some of the things that she
has said make me feel that she doesn't really understand what
happened that day. I haven't explained too much to Michele,
because I thought it would upset her even more, but I thought
you should know."

"I appreciate that." There were a few silent seconds and then
she continued.

"That day," Barbara shuddered and dabbed her eyes. "That day was so unnerving to begin with. I was supposed to pick up Michele and Josh and take them to my house. The plan was that I would take care of Josh and she would rest. It would sort of give both her and Jeff the day off."

I nodded.

"Well, it was pouring, so I called Michele about ten and said I didn't think it would be a good idea to take Josh out in the rain. Normally Michele would have been the first one to suggest that." Barbara lowered her head for a moment, then looked up again. "Dr. Burak, you never knew Michele before this. I'm not sure she'll ever be the same, but she was the gentlest, kindest, most loving human being on the face of this earth. She loved kids and they loved her. She was always taking care of her friends' children. My son Tony is thirteen and she is one of his favorite people. He knows what happened, but it's remarkable how he insists that something must have been wrong with Michele. He just won't get angry. He is unshakable."

I nodded again.

"Sorry, I got off track."

"Barbara, nothing is off track, and I really appreciate that you're here. I know how hard this must be."

She nodded, and then continued. "Even before I said we shouldn't bring Josh out in the weather she sounded strange."

"What do you mean?"

"Well, her voice had no emotion, it was absolutely flat—almost a monotone. Then when we weren't going out she didn't seem upset, yet I knew she was. I told her that Buster, my dog, had thrown up on the living room carpet and I had to shampoo it. She hardly responded. After I hung up I had this feeling that the carpet could wait. I called her back to let her know that I was coming right away."

"So you went over in the morning?"

"Yeah, I stayed for about six hours."

"Interesting—because I'm sure Michele told me that you came in the afternoon for about an hour."

"Really? Well she was so out of it that day. When I arrived she was just sitting on the back porch in the dark. Jeff was there and he said, 'Michele, why don't you turn on the light?' She didn't answer. So I turned on the light and right away she asked me if I would turn it off, told me that the light bothered her— and there's something else that I wanted you to know. Michele didn't think she could take care of Josh very well, but I watched her for the few weeks before and she actually did a pretty good job. But that day really was different, she was so stiff with him, I really had to do most of his care. At one point she even said something about how good I was with him and how inept she was. I tried very hard to reassure her."

"But you don't think she really heard you?"

"No. I couldn't seem to get through. Jeff came in and I made lunch for the three of us. I don't think she ate. She just seemed incapable of doing almost anything at that point."

"You made lunch?"

I didn't say anything, but I also remembered Michele telling me that she made a sandwich for Jeff. I wondered what else she hadn't remembered accurately. "Barbara, did Michele say anything to you about taking Joshua with you?"

The young woman across from me began to cry again. She shook her head yes, unable to get out the words. It took a few moments. "I can't sleep without the light on anymore, and I can't be alone in the house. I have nightmares—I should have taken him. I feel so guilty, but I just didn't know. I just didn't know."

I waited for a few moments until Barbara stopped sobbing and blew her nose. As gently as I could, I asked, "Why do you think she asked you to take him?" I held my breath.

"Well, I thought it was because she felt so inadequate that she felt she couldn't take care of him."

"Do you think she had any thoughts of hurting Josh and that's why she asked you?"

Barbara looked me in the eye. "No. Absolutely not. I've thought since then that Michele may have already decided she was going to use the gun, and she wanted me to take Josh so he wouldn't be alone after she did it. I just don't know. But I still don't believe she was thinking about hurting him at all, just herself. But I can't stop thinking that I should have taken him, I can't stop the thoughts."

"Tell me something, Barbara, if you had the slightest inkling, the faintest notion that something would happen to Michele, or to Josh, could you have walked out?"

"No. Never."

"I think you're right; there's just no way that any rational person could have known."

I hoped our conversation was a help, but I figured her nightmares would continue, at least for a while.

# 23 🍂

By the early afternoon streets had become rivers and the gloomy day was punctuated by lightning and thunder. At about one-thirty Jeff went inside to dry off again, to have a cup of coffee and to check on Michele and Josh. Barbara was there and everything seemed fine. Shortly after returning to work he was surprised when his brother Chris, who lived next door, came outside to join him. It seemed that being cooped up with five young children was less appealing than being out in the rain.

At about four-thirty Jeff and Chris decided to take a break. They each headed for their respective pots of coffee. Michele was in the kitchen when Jeff came through the door and hung his slicker on a hook. She didn't say anything.

"I didn't notice Barbara leave."

"Yeah—she had to go—but I was glad she came."

Jeff went to the coffee. "What's for dinner?"

"I don't know, what would you like?"

"Do we have any chicken?"

"Yes."

"How about baked chicken?"

Michele hesitated a second. "Okay."

Jeff poured a cup of coffee and turned around and set it on the kitchen table. "I'm going to check on Josh for a second."

Walking to his son's room, he had a fleeting thought that

Michele really didn't seem better. There was almost no decision involved as he pushed that thought aside, not wanting to even open the door to the possibility that she was going to be in her slump again. He watched his son sleeping peacefully and felt content, with just the slightest hint of uncertainty. After a quick bathroom stop he was back to the kitchen. The coffee was hot and tasted good.

"Want another?" Michele asked.

"No, thanks—I want to finish a few things before the light is gone."

Jeff put the now empty cup in the sink. As he began to put on his raincoat Michele said, "I need to talk to you." Jeff looked at his wife. There seemed to be no urgency in her voice and she was calm, not particularly upset.

"Sure, honey, let me finish a few things and we'll talk at dinner." Michele did not protest.

There is no way of calculating how many times Jeff wished he could have that moment back.

Immediately after Jeff returned to the backyard Chris reappeared. By five-fifteen, however, he had enough and returned to the warmth of his living room; Jeff was determined to stay until the light gave out entirely.

It must have been about 5:50 P.M. that there was a tremendous clap of thunder and the lights all around went out. Power outages during a storm are commonplace in Bennington and Jeff knew that Michele did not like being alone in the dark. He began to pack up.

During the minute or two it took to put his tools in a safe, dry place in the barn, the lights returned. It was then that he noticed that his own house was still dark. Strange. He felt a small prickle at the back of his neck and walked quickly through the sodden backyard to the kitchen door. The knob turned but the door did not budge. Now the prickle became electric. He ran to the front door. Bolted!

Suddenly frantic, Jeff ran again to the backdoor, which had a weaker latch. At the instant that his boot slammed to the right of the knob, lightning split the sky and illuminated the scene. The wood cracked, freeing the latch, and the door flew open.

Crashing through the kitchen in the dark, Jeff knocked something over. His hand flicked out to the familiar switch next to the doorway between the kitchen and the living room. The sixty-watt bulb in the kitchen fixture gave just enough light into the living room for Jeff to see.

For a fleeting instant he had the feeling that he had stepped into a puzzle: "Something is wrong with this picture." Michele was sitting in the Lazy Boy chair, not moving. He bounded across the room. "Michele!" No response. "What's wrong?" He heard only the sound of her moan. He took his wife by the shoulders and shook her. "What's wrong?!" He was in a panic. Michele did not open her eyes, she just moaned more. It was then he saw the baby seat. Life stopped.

The moment seemed to go on forever. Every detail was unavoidable and impossible. Joshua was sitting in a baby seat on the coffee table. He didn't move a muscle. But what Jeff noticed most of all was his color. He was white. Not Caucasian—but white like typewriter paper.

# 24 🍂

Carrie Remington heard someone pounding on the front door. She opened the door and saw her brother-in-law breathing into Joshua's mouth. "Chris," she screamed, nothing more. He appeared almost instantly and seconds later the brothers were running to his car. As they got in, Chris turned back and yelled to his wife, "Call the hospital." Carrie watched them leave, then picked up the phone.

The trip to the hospital from 112 Jefferson Street is short; three blocks to Weeks, then right for six blocks, then north again on Dewey for half a block to the hospital driveway. "Nothing made sense," Jeff would recall. Here we were speeding to the hospital, but as I held Joshua I somehow knew he would never breathe again. My mind was indescribably confused. Then I saw the blood and the hole in Joshua's clothing. All of a sudden it clicked. Michele shot Joshua—then she shot herself.

Sue Lavender happened to be the closest to the emergency room phone when it rang. At the other end of the line Carrie was speaking rapidly. "My husband is driving his brother and the baby to the hospital. The baby's not breathing."

Sue asked, "When will they arrive?"

"In a minute," Carrie said.

"How old is the baby and do you know what's wrong?"

"Joshua's about six weeks old—but I don't know what's wrong—except he was very sick when he was born and had to go to Albany. I know he gets medicine every day."

"Anything else?"

"No."

"Well, thanks very much." Sue swung into action.

Six o'clock on a Saturday evening, usually a quiet time when most of the hospital staff is at home enjoying the weekend. But on that Saturday evening, purely by chance, a remarkably appropriate group of professionals were in the building.

Dr. Ben Rogers, chief of emergency services at the Southwestern Vermont Medical Center (SVMC), was just finishing his day shift in the emergency department. Coming on duty for the long Saturday night was Dr. Richard Stern, the only emergency physician at SVMC who was also a board certified pediatrician (an unusual combination).

Sue Lavender summoned both physicians and explained the situation. Instinct and experience led Ben Rogers to call upstairs to the operating suite. A young man had come in earlier with what appeared to be appendicitis. Ben knew that Fred Loy was probably finished operating but might still be in the building. He was, along with Dr. Silvio Pescati, the anesthesiologist who had worked with Fred during the surgery. Ben explained, "We have a situation here—baby coming in not breathing—I don't know what's going on, could you hang around for a few minutes?" Both doctors were about to go home for dinner. Instead they went downstairs to the emergency department.

Richard Stern called Adam Richards, the chief respiratory therapist who also was on campus that evening. Adam was on his way to the emergency department as soon as he had the phone back in its cradle.

Liz Gold, the charge nurse in the emergency department, had been standing next to Sue when the call from Carrie Remington came in. Liz didn't know whether the "not breathing baby" was alive or dead, unconscious or awake, choking, seizing, or drowning. The thought that the baby might have been shot never crossed her mind; she had absolutely no idea that the baby's mother was sitting in her living room with a bullet in her chest. It was just instinct that led her to pick up the phone and call the hospital nursing supervisor Jean Brooks. Within thirty seconds, Jean was also on her way to the emergency department.

The third emergency department nurse on duty that evening was twenty-six-year-old Mary Bragdon. Pretty, with short brown hair and an engaging smile, Mary had recently returned to work after her own maternity leave. Her four-month-old son, her first born, was happily at home with her husband Jim. For Mary and Jim, Brad's birth had been a wonderful experience, and the weeks that followed had been filled with the joy that most couples expect after the baby arrives. It was Mary who happened to be standing closest to the automatic doors that lead out to the ambulance bay as Chris Remington's car careened into the space. Mary was not prepared for the next thirty seconds of her life. No one would have been.

Chris and Jeff, carrying his son, and continuing to try to do mouth-to-mouth resuscitation while running, barely allowed the sliding glass doors to open before they crashed through, almost knocking Mary over. Jeff yelled something that sounded like "shot!"

Mary asked, "What did you say?"

"My baby's been shot—my wife shot the baby and then shot herself."

As he spoke he passed Joshua's body into the arms of this young mother. Mary took one quick look at Josh, sheet-white with the bullet wound in his chest. The implications of the moment were too far-reaching and dramatic for her to stop or react emotionally. Later she would be profoundly upset. At that moment she was an emergency department nurse.

Even though he was younger and smaller, Joshua's limp body seemed much heavier than that of her own son whom she had held in her arms just a few hours earlier. Mary ran to the trauma room. Despite the absence of all signs of life, the activity was frantic. It continued for about fifteen minutes until Fred Loy, who had arrived from the operating suite, called the team's efforts to a halt.

After Carrie Remington called the hospital she ran next door to her sister-in-law. In the low light she saw Michele sitting in the Lazy Boy, her head back, her arms across her chest. She was saying over and over, "I don't care, let me die." Carrie asked her if she had taken anything, and tried to get her to move. Michele said, "Leave me alone, it hurts." Frightened and not understanding what was happening, Carrie decided to call her father-in-law. Glenn Remington usually knew what to do. While she was on the phone with Glenn, Chris Remington was calling the police from the hospital. The time was 6:09 P.M.

Jimmy Bogo, on duty for the Bennington Rescue Squad, was in the police station when the call came in. He and Sgt. Mike Breen jumped into a police cruiser and rushed to 112 Jefferson, only three blocks away. Seth Bogo, Jimmy's brother, and other rescue squad members were beeped. It seems that most of the people in Bennington were sitting by their police scanners as though it was old-time radio. By 6:11 P.M. many people were aware of the developing drama.

Jimmy Bogo is an assistant manager of a local supermarket. Personable and intelligent, he had volunteered for rescue squad work in 1982, gone through the required training, and had in addition displayed a distinctive knack for doing the right thing, something that cannot be taught.

"When we walked into that darkened living room it took a second to focus," he remembers. "Then I saw the figure of a woman slumped in a chair. I went over and quietly asked her name, but she didn't identify herself, mumbling only, 'My chest hurts.' I tried to find out what was wrong but she was holding her chest tightly and didn't want to move her hands. Then she looked at me and said, 'Let me die—it's not supposed to happen this way.' "

While Jimmy was trying to help Michele, his brother Seth came through the front door. Within two minutes Karen Wiley and George Prescott, the third and fourth members of the team, arrived in the ambulance. At about the same time two additional police vehicles, each containing two police officers, pulled up in front of the house. The ambulance was parked across the street.

There were now eleven people in the Remington living room: four rescue workers, five police officers, Carrie Remington, and Michele. Overwhelmed by the confusion and with the full rescue team present, Michele resisted no more. The squad members were able to identify the source of pain—a gunshot wound in the left chest area.

They efficiently moved Michele to a stretcher and gently rolled her on her right side. There was no exit wound—the bullet was still somewhere in her body and it was clear that she was very weak.

During the brief ride to the hospital Michele remained conscious. She pleaded with the rescue squad workers, "Let me die— let me die." While her pleas echoed in the metallic confines of the ambulance, additional help was being summoned in the hospital. Three experienced nurses, two from the intensive care unit and one from a general medical nursing unit, were riding the elevator to emergency. Having received word via radio that the baby's mother had a gunshot wound to the chest, Dr. Loy also asked that Dr. Robert Pearson, fellow surgeon and hospital chief of staff, be called in to assist him. Bob arrived within five minutes.

If the scene in the Remington living room had been a gathering, the scene at the emergency department at that time appeared to be a convention. At least twenty-nine people were there when Michele's stretcher was wheeled through the door. In addition to the hospital personnel, the rescue workers, and the police, Michele's father-in-law had arrived as well as her parents, both of whom were in tears.

The rescue efforts with Joshua had just ended as Michele was brought in. Mary Bragdon, the same nurse who had carried Joshua's limp body to the trauma room, made the first move toward Michele.

# 25 🍂

My days are often long. I leave before my son goes to school in the morning and return home after dark, usually with phone calls to make. It's difficult to spend much time with Eli during the week except on Wednesday afternoons when I don't schedule patients.

On winter Wednesdays I try to join his school's ski program. During the fall and spring when there is no skiing he arrives home early and we often have lunch and spend the afternoon together. Wednesday, April 8, was typical except that I didn't see Michele that morning and I didn't want to miss a day. So somewhere between my third and fourth slice of pizza, I said, "After lunch I have to go back to the hospital for a while."

"Will you be long?"

"Probably about an hour." Eli didn't ask me why I had to go back to the hospital, he just said, "Okay."

"Do you have any homework?"

"A little."

"Why don't you do it and we'll do something when I get back."

At the age of almost nine he still listened.

As we finished lunch I watched my son with special awareness. I felt so lucky and so sad at the same time.

\* \* \*

During that first week my meetings with Michele were quiet, sad, without profound revelations. We were building trust on a trickle of small talk and I hoped we had that chemistry that would allow us to really connect. If we did, time would be my ally.

After I dropped Eli at home I returned to the hospital, which was only four minutes away. Michele was very tired and our discussion was brief. I left her to a long nap. As I was writing a note in her chart, Ellen Goldman and Michael Brent again approached in tandem. "We've had a chance to work with Michele now for a few days," Ellen said. "She seems tired, sad, yet in a way so," she paused searching for the right word, "so normal. We've been reading your notes. Do you really think she can't remember what happened?"

"I don't know. No one can really go into someone else's mind. So I guess it's possible that she remembers more than she is saying but I don't think so."

Mike chimed in, "Well, it's hard to believe that she really doesn't remember something like this."

There was an intensity in his voice and I could see that both of them were troubled. Probably a lot of people were.

"Got a few minutes?" I asked. They nodded. I motioned to some empty chairs nearby. They sat and I continued, "I don't think anyone knows exactly how the mind manipulates memory. You've seen people who have had amnesia because of head trauma or some other serious injury?" They both nodded. "Well, Michele shot herself and was in shock when she came in, so it's not farfetched that she might not remember much of what happened during that time—but I think that's only part of the story." Both Ellen and Mike were quiet. "The world is too complex for any of us to operate every minute of every day totally aware of everything. We're all on automatic pilot a great deal of the time. What any of us are actually conscious of is just the tip of the iceberg. Don't you use the term subconscious or unconscious?" They nodded again.

"So let's just say that for all of us what is remembered or forgotten is not always a matter of how well we've recorded something; it has to do with the meaning of that particular event in your life. I think Michele's difficulty in remembering has to do with the emotional impact of what she did." Ellen and Mike both had a glassed-over look in their eyes at that point. I felt as though I had lost them.

I had been thinking a lot about this subject during the past few days but hadn't really discussed my thoughts with anyone. I continued again, "Have either of you ever had the experience of someone reminding you of something that happened that involved you, which sounded important but you didn't remember it?"

Ellen closed her eyes, pursed her lips in almost a smile and began nodding her head. "As a matter of fact, when I saw my brother last Thanksgiving he was talking about something that happened when I was nine. I had no idea what he was talking about, then he reminded me with a couple of embarrassing details. I remember saying to myself 'How could I have forgotten?'"

I continued again. "You know, this happened a great deal during the Vietnam War. A lot of men who returned had witnessed atrocities and participated in events that are hard to imagine. Some of these men continue to have trouble psychologically and sometimes it is only after a long time that they remember what is stirring up the pot. Sometimes they don't ever remember."

Mike's memory was triggered. "You know, I saw a film about some intense group therapy that was being done at Stanford with Vietnam veterans. The therapist and the group were being tough on one guy. I'm not sure what he remembered but suddenly he opened up. He was sobbing and overwhelmed. It was pretty dramatic, but the implication was that remembering led to some sort of emotional healing. If that's true and if Michele really can't remember, would forcing her to remember be good for her?"

I hesitated. "I really don't know, Mike. Just as there are some things better left unsaid, there may be some memories that are better left buried."

Mary Bragdon never remembered dreams, but two nights after Joshua's body had been placed in her arms by Jeff Remington, Mary awakened from a nightmare. In this vivid creation of her mind Michele was wheeled into the emergency department—pale, dead, with fangs that were covered with blood.

Mary doesn't think she made a sound as she awakened. She remembers only that she was sitting up in bed, half in the dream, half out—with tears streaming down her face. This moment of confusion was interrupted by her husband's voice, which at first startled her but quickly brought her back to reality. Normally Jim would sleep through anything, even their own baby's nighttime cries, but now he was up.

"Honey, what's wrong? Is the baby okay?"

"Our baby's okay—but I had a dream about the baby who was brought into the emergency room Saturday night."

Jim reached for his wife and put his arm around her shoulders. The incident troubled him greatly. The love he felt for his infant son was so strong he couldn't imagine the possibility that a parent could take his child's life. When Mary first told him, his words had been, "That woman must be totally out of her mind."

Mary cried softly for a minute, maybe two. Then, as though there was some sort of silent communication between them, both felt a need to check Kevin. Getting out of bed they walked together to the baby's room. He was fine, peaceful and angelic. The young couple stood quietly at his bedside for about five minutes just watching. Back in their own room they talked for a while longer until the sandman sprinkled more of his dust.

On Thursday, April 9, the morning after Mary's nightmare, I arrived at the hospital at about six-fifteen. From Dewey Street, the brick building appears stately and serene sitting on a grassy knoll framed by the mountains behind. As I drove up the long driveway the brick was warmly lit by that special orange of the morning sun. The grass was wet and sparkled. The mountains themselves, still early April brown except for evergreen patches, were quite beautiful with their own orange cloak.

I thought of the other places I had worked in years past. Other hospitals framed by city streets, large buildings, noise, and dirt—and I remembered why I had moved here.

The doctors' parking lot was almost empty. There was only one vehicle, a gray minivan, which I knew belonged to one of the obstetricians. In all likelihood Bennington's population had grown by one during the night.

Including Michele I had four patients to see, three of whom were in the special management, or psychiatric, unit. That was my first stop. The night nursing staff reported that all had been quiet. One of my patients was awake and we sat in the kitchen area quietly talking for about twenty minutes before other patients began to drift in. By seven forty-five I had spoken with each of my patients in SMU; I headed for Michele's room in the intensive care unit.

Michele greeted me immediately when I entered her room. She seemed more alert and the number of tubes and wires connected to her body had diminished. We had barely begun to speak when Dr. Loy entered the room. Finding me with Michele and not wanting to intrude, he was about to leave, but I motioned him to stay.

"I didn't want to interrupt," he said.

"That's okay, Fred—no problem."

Dr. Loy turned to Michele. "Well, how are you feeling this morning?"

"Okay."

"Any new pain or difficulty breathing?"

"Nope."

"Could you sit up for a second so I can listen to your back?"

Michele sat and Dr. Loy moved his stethoscope to different areas, then had her lie down so he could check her incisions.

"Everything seems pretty good," he said. "Probably tomorrow we can get you out of intensive care."

Michele nodded passively. Fred and I glanced briefly at each other before he said, "I'll see you later this afternoon, Michele," and then he left.

About fifteen minutes after Fred Loy left my beeper went off. The beeper is like a long leash that has me permanently conditioned. Even when I am not wearing it, even when I am two thousand miles away, if a beeper pitch is part of music or generated in some other way I often flinch slightly. After the beeps, the disembodied voice from my belt said, "Would you please call Ms. Mullin at extension 492."

Before I answered the page I spent a few more minutes with Michele. I explained to her that I would be in Boston for a conference the next day and had to leave very early in the morning, so I wouldn't be able to see her.

"I'm sorry you won't be in tomorrow, but I'll see you over the weekend?"

I was surprised and pleased by the question. This was the first time that Michele had given me the slightest clue that my visits mattered.

"Sure, I'll be here."

\* \* \*

Muriel Mullin of extension 492 was the head nurse in the hospital. In her mid-thirties, good natured, efficient, she seemed married to her career. When I returned her call she asked if we could meet briefly before I left the hospital.

"Sure," I said, "where are you?"

"Downstairs in the president's office."

The president's office is located on the ground floor near the doctors' entrance. The medical library is located just across the hall from that office and I suggested we meet there in five minutes.

Muriel got right to the point. "I'm a little worried about the nurses who were in the emergency department on the night that Michele Remington was brought in. A few of them are not sleeping well and almost everyone who was there has come to me during this past week wanting to talk. Mostly they want to understand how something like this could happen. So I was wondering if you would be willing to spend some time talking with the nurses who were there that night—maybe a group meeting?"

I had some immediate concerns. It first had to do with Michele's privacy. In psychiatry, probably more than any other specialty, secrets are sacred. Knowing you can come to another human being free to say whatever you like without the fear that it could be whispered down the lane is very special and important. The only time I would knowingly violate this trust of confidentiality would be to save a life (the patient's or someone else whom the patient specifically threatened) or when required by law, and even then there might be some discretion over what I would say or would not say.

The second area of concern was one I always had when speaking to a group of people who were upset about something. I would be talking blind, not really sure how each person might react to what I was saying, or what personal concerns I might be touching.

Despite these issues, however, I did want to speak to the

nurses. I knew most of them well and wanted to help. I also had some sense of what they might be feeling as I remembered my own initial anger. I also saw this invitation as an opportunity to practice a little preventive psychiatry. Here was a group of reasonable professionals who were not waiting until their upset grew and their symptoms became worse, but were trying instead to nip a problem in the bud.

"I'd be happy to meet with the group—but even though Michele's situation is quite public I need to be careful about some of the discussion where her privacy is concerned."

"We've thought about that and certainly respect your relationship with her," Muriel said, "but I know that this discussion would be helpful."

The meeting was scheduled for 2:00 P.M. on Wednesday, April 15. The next morning as I drove to Boston, I found myself thinking a lot about what I might say.

# 26 ~

It was Friday, April 10, six days after the shooting, when I first raised the issue with Michele. I had already come to think of her as a very candid person. She didn't mince words. "Well," she said, "I haven't been thinking about it except that I've tried twice and just screwed things up—so I'm not about to try to kill myself again." I think I felt more comfortable, but I wasn't about to curl up and go to sleep. There were miles to go and I would have to be continually watchful.

Walking out of Michele's room following that conversation I saw Fred Loy approaching. I was reminded that he had been a champion diver during his high school and college years; the grace was evident in his movement. Slightly shorter than I, his gaze was upward as he spoke. "Michele is doing surprisingly well. She'll be transferred out of intensive care today. From my standpoint she might have to stay in the hospital for a few more days, but beyond that it's your call." I think I just shook my head and did not share my soul-searching, which had already begun.

No one would have questioned a recommendation for a lengthier psychiatric stay, either in our hospital or somewhere else. I just wasn't sure that it was needed or that it was in Michele's best interest. "Fred, do you have any objections to transferring Michele to SMU?"

"No, I'd be happy to do that."

The main reason I wanted Michele in SMU was not because of her behavior or confusion, but because I would receive especially helpful feedback from the nurses. In addition to their experience and comfort with psychological issues, their job both allowed and required that they spend a great deal more time talking with patients than the nurses on the medical and surgical units who have to spend most of their time dispensing medications, dressing wounds, managing IVs, and ministering to the many physical needs of general hospital patients.

Michele was not thrilled with the transfer; neither was Jeff. Incredibly, despite all that had happened, the idea of being placed in the psychiatric unit was uncomfortable for both. They cooperated but felt uneasy.

The second morning after Michele was transferred Anna Rosario approached me as soon as I walked on to the unit. She is a bright, sensitive young woman from the Philippines who had just been named supervising nurse.

"Good morning," she said pleasantly.

"Morning Anna, how are you?"

"Good." She paused. "I wanted to talk with you about Michele Remington."

"What do you think?"

"Well, it's as though she's in a fog. There is a certain amount of denial about what happened, but we all think that she really understands to some extent—yet it's confusing."

"You think she actually remembers?"

"I don't know—I don't think so."

"I know what you mean," I said. "It's hard to be sure just what she remembers or understands."

"And you know," Anna said, "there's something else that's interesting. She's really sad, so quiet, but I suspect she is less depressed or psychotic or whatever than before this happened."

I agreed.

In the weeks before Joshua had been shot, Michele's depression had clearly distorted her view of the world. There had been little emotion in her relationship with her son, no confidence that she could function as a mother, no value placed on her own existence, and no hope for the future. She couldn't sleep, didn't care to eat and felt paralyzed by lack of energy. She was even hallucinating. Now, in the hospital, after being shot herself, after the death of her son, she was somewhat better. Although fogbound and certainly not lighthearted, according to Jeff and her parents she was not as profoundly altered as she had been before the tragedy. Why? I didn't know.

I doubt this lessening of depression was due to the antidepressant medication that I had started. She had been taking it only for a few days and usually this sort of medication requires a few weeks to work.

Perhaps the physical trauma of the shooting, the unconsciousness, the surgery, had in some way conspired to improve her emotional condition—sort of a self-inflicted shock therapy. Perhaps the denial that protected her from totally comprehending what had happened allowed her to go on.

Michele was sleeping and eating better than she had been. Her physical recovery was going well, and she expected that she would soon be able to leave the hospital. That's what she wanted to do.

On Monday morning Jeff approached me. Unlike his wife, he was emotionally unprotected. There was no fog, no denial, no numbness protecting his soul. Where Michele was vague, he was crystal clear and painfully explicit. Every moment of the day of tragedy was burned into his memory. Yet the anger that had exploded two days earlier had already passed. He had become increasingly attentive. In his mind Michele was a victim; she had been "sick." This he fervently believed. He had to. He had already lost Joshua and he couldn't lose his wife as well. He became Michele's advocate, but he was speaking for himself also when he said, "Michele's not comfortable here—she wants to be at home so we can be together. I don't think it will help her to stay. I think she'll do better if she is able to move back into her life in a more normal way."

In a sense I agreed with Jeff. Staying in the hospital would not necessarily speed up the work of therapy. This was going to take a very long time. At some point, however, Michele could be hit with the full impact of what she had done—perhaps she would even remember. Then anything could happen. The problem was I didn't know and couldn't know whether this might be sooner or later. It could be weeks, months, or even longer before total reality came crashing in—if it ever did.

Perhaps having her stay in the hospital and keeping "the pressure on" would cause this day of reckoning to come sooner, but I wasn't at all sure that this was in Michele's best interest. I really wanted to allow her to do whatever she could to rediscover her life in as normal a way as possible (realizing of course that "normal" would probably never be the same again).

In the final analysis I placed more value on giving Michele the message that her terrible deed did not represent who she was nor who she would be. I decided in the long run it would be better for her to go home.

This was one of the most difficult clinical decisions I've ever had to make. There was not a single person associated closely with Michele who was not concerned about her rapid departure from the hospital. Nonetheless, on April 14, just ten days after the worst day of her life, Michele went home.

"I'll watch her like a hawk," Jeff said.

I knew he would. But even so, hawks have to sleep.

# 27 🍂

I'd thought a lot about this meeting.

Mary Bragdon, Sue Lavender, and Elizabeth Gold were in the emergency room on the night of April 4. Elise Fender had come over to help from maternity. She had also worked with Michele during her postpartum stay. Jean Brooks, the night supervisor, spent a lot of time in emergency that fateful Saturday evening. Michael Brent, the head nurse in intensive care, had also been there, as well as having taken care of Michele after her surgery. Finally, Ellen Goldman knew Michele only from intensive care. Eight glum faces if you counted mine.

The lounge adjacent to the emergency department was almost too small for this group but it was the best we could do, especially since Sue and Liz were on duty and had to be close. Although two "floaters" were covering for a few hours, Sue and Liz could be called if it became too busy. Hopefully, however, on a Wednesday afternoon in spring that wouldn't happen.

The room was a typical emergency department lounge: sofa, chairs, desk, refrigerator, microwave, and the obligatory coffee machine. Although I had not been in this room often, it had a very familiar and comfortable feel. For ten years before becoming a psychiatrist I had worked as an emergency physician and spent many hours in similar rooms in various hospitals in Pennsylvania and California.

For the most part we all knew each other pretty well. There was no need for introductions. I said quietly, "How can I help?— Or rather how can we help each other?"

There was a brief silence when everyone looked around nervously for a few seconds. Then Sue Lavender began. "You know, I've worked in this ER for about six years. During that time I've seen awful things—children having seizures, suicide attempts, wife beatings. I've been with drunk patients who were horrible to me personally. I've seen the most terrible accidents—I thought I'd seen it all—and through it all I felt professional. I was a nurse and my job was in perspective. Yet that night—when the baby was brought in—and they brought in Michele—shot, maybe dying, I really had to struggle—I didn't tell anyone at the time but I was so angry and upset I just wanted to let her suffer. And I still feel as though I've lost something. Somehow I'm a little different with everyone in a way that I can't explain but I don't like it." She paused.

I looked around. Almost imperceptibly heads were nodding in agreement. I understood all too well; the memory of my own anger when Fred first called me was still fresh. These thoughts remained private at that moment, however, because Liz Gold responded before I uttered a word.

"Sue, I think we understand. It was just a mess. I felt the same way but I did what I had to do. We all did."

Almost without a pause Mary Bragdon began to speak. "I think I was in shock. Here this man hands me a baby and I knew he was dead—but at the same time I didn't know—didn't want to know. I just ran to the trauma room and must have been on automatic until a few minutes later when I saw Michele being wheeled in. That's when the whole thing really hit me. I could only think of my own baby and just couldn't understand—how—how . . ." Mary's face became red. She slashed her hand along the countertop near the sofa where she was sitting and a few magazines landed on the floor. Liz reached over and placed her hand gently across Mary's shoulders. Mary continued, "I've been like this—so angry and upset one minute and then just hugging my baby for minutes at a time." Mary looked at me. "Can I get over my anger and this feeling that something is somehow so wrong—so out of whack?" She paused for just a spilt second. Then she said, "You told me earlier in the week that you too had been very upset. How do you feel now? You've been seeing Michele—I know you've seen the family—you know more than we do—does it make a difference?"

Mary was now about a word away from tears. I said quietly, "I can't say how it would be for anyone else, but it's been a help for me to be able to spend time with Michele and Jeff and her mother and father. Maybe it's a little easier because I never actually saw Joshua"—I hesitated. "How do I feel now? Well, heartsick is about the best word. I feel terrible about the baby, about Jeff and his parents and Michele's parents, but now I also feel badly for Michele." No one said a word. I continued, "This does not feel like other cases, like other difficult situations I've been involved with—this is consuming. It's been constantly in my thoughts and I've felt a little overwhelmed and lost."

I glanced around and every pair of eyes met mine. We were all together in this and there was no room for superficial support or platitudes. Hopefully, each of us would take something from this meeting that would help. I looked at Mary, who seemed a bit more relaxed, or maybe that was my imagination. I continued. "I know everyone's been talking about this all week. What do you think happened?"

Elise Fender had been sitting quietly on my left. I knew her well. She was an especially sensitive young woman and I was somehow very aware of her presence and I wasn't quite sure why. She had taken care of Michele during her stay in maternity, but I happened to know that she was the only one of us who knew Michele before the shooting. She spoke with a strained quality at first, as if her throat was tight.

"I think we've all heard the same thing—that Michele was suffering from postpartum depression. I've heard the words postpartum depression more in the past week than I have in the past few years working on maternity. I'm not sure what that means anymore." She paused briefly as if to gather herself together. "I haven't been able to sleep. I know her. I can't understand. I can't imagine her doing this."

Liz Gold looked as if she were about to say something, but I managed to catch her eye and shook my head no. I knew Elise had not finished.

"I just don't know what to think. Michèle was depressed, but I've seen a number of other women who were. It was unusual that she stayed when the baby went to Albany—but she seemed too frightened to be transferred, or even to go for a visit. But she was such a nice person." Tears were beginning to well up. Elise tried to blink them back. "I just can't even think . . ." The blinking failed. Tears spilled out, tracing small rivers down her pretty cheeks. She began to sob. My eyes began to fill and my throat became tight. Other eyes were moist. We were all silent, all comfortable being uncomfortable. Finally I could talk. I directed a question to Elise that had been on my mind for a few days.

"Did Michele seem better by the time she left the hospital?"

"A little bit—but not completely." Elise was regaining her composure. "She almost needed to be talked into leaving the hospital. I think she was still frightened about taking care of Joshua, but we couldn't get her to really talk about it. I knew— we all knew—that she was uneasy but she tried to put up a good front. So she went home and now I feel horrible. Maybe if I had pushed Dr. Murray harder he would have kept her, or asked you to see her."

"You did tell him your concerns?" I asked.

"Yes, I told him," Elise said, "but I still wish I had tried harder."

"Hindsight is always easier, but you did absolutely what you had to do!" I was emphatic. "Elise, hindsight makes everything look so clear but the world doesn't work that way. Getting a psych consult was Dr. Murray's decision, and you suggested it. And there is no way you could have known this was going to happen. In fact, that's part of the reality of this—in the course of a busy obstetrician's life so many women get the blues after a baby is born that it almost becomes routine. The more serious depressions get lumped in with the baby blues and are not always appreciated. But this—what happened to Michele—is just so outrageous—it just never happens. It's hard to believe it could. There was just no way you could ever have predicted, so stop beating yourself up!"

Even as I was speaking I knew that no matter how sincere my words, Elise would continue to struggle. Pain and self-questioning is just part of being in medicine and taking responsibility for life and death situations. I handed her a box of Kleenex. She took a few tissues and blotted her face and blew her nose. Liz moved a bit closer and gave Elise a gentle hug. We were all quiet. For a few moments there was silence. The room was very still. And we were all surprised by what Ellen Goldman had to say.

Ellen Goldman had lived in Bridgeport, Connecticut, while her children were young and she had worked only part time. With her children grown, after she moved to Bennington she returned to full-time intensive care nursing. She began, "This all seems like a long time ago but I've been thinking about it a lot this past week. After I had my daughter Julie I went through a very hard time. It didn't start out that way. At first everything was wonderful, but then after a few weeks I began to feel worse. At first I didn't want to admit how I was feeling but I was angry, irritable, and weepy. My husband knew something was wrong.

At the time my son was three and I had enjoyed him as a baby so I thought the second time around would be even easier—but it wasn't. It just didn't make any sense, but no matter what I did I couldn't shake it. Bill finally spoke to my obstetrician who said that some women do become depressed for a while and . . . I've never said this to anyone before . . . at times with Julie I had these thoughts—more like fears—that I might somehow hurt her, that I might drop her or something. I didn't think it would happen, but I was so scared and felt so guilty for even thinking such things." She began to cry.

Liz Gold was sitting close to Ellen and she motioned to Mary to pass along the box of tissues. Ellen looked at me. "I've been so ashamed for even having those thoughts. But since this happened with Michele I've been frightened. Could I have lost control?"

I hesitated. "You didn't."

"Thank God for that," Ellen said. "But what saved me—what happened to Michele that didn't happen to me?"

Ellen's honesty made things easier for me. In the space of thirty seconds her surprising and personal disclosure transformed the feeling in the room. There was less anger—more concern—more softness, I guess is the best word. I had been thinking that some of what I might say could seem protective of Michele and not truly objective. Now I felt that everyone would be listening with Ellen in mind and I would be heard with more openness.

"Ellen is the third woman this week who told me that in their postpartum they had thoughts of hurting their baby. The other two women were former patients who called because they heard about Michele's situation and my involvement. They seemed to want to confess these feelings they had been carrying around for a long time. They had always felt guilty, and like Ellen neither woman had ever told anyone about this before, not even their husbands."

I watched Ellen; a look of absolute incredulity crossed her face.

When we learn that our worst private thoughts or moments are not unique, that others have experienced similar pain or similar distasteful flights of fancy, it is sometimes very reassuring.

I looked around the room. "I want to ask you all a few questions—and I am not trying to embarrass anyone—I'm just trying to sort out what happened and maybe make it clearer if that's possible. If this is too personal just say so." Everyone was silent and waiting.

"How many of you have ever been depressed?"

It took a few seconds, then hands began to move skyward like stalks of corn. First two, then four, then everyone; a crop of seven hands. I raised my own hand to make eight. "I'm not surprised because at some time all of us feel down or sad or what we call 'depressed.' But I have a hunch about something—what if I asked how many of you went through a period of time when you had no energy to do anything—when you slept poorly or maybe too much but no matter how much or how little you slept you got up in the morning not rested—a time you couldn't get motivated at all, couldn't seem to make decisions and generally felt hopeless—when the whole world was gray—when you couldn't quite think clearly, couldn't concentrate, couldn't read a book or watch TV, forgot things easily? How many maybe even thought of suicide? How many here have ever gone through some or all of that—whether for a few days or longer?"

Mike Brent's hand went up immediately, followed by Sue's, then Ellen's. The rest remained down.

"Maybe some of you would disagree, but I think it's almost impossible to understand the way life is paralyzed with major depression unless you've been there. When someone is at their worst, simple things are just impossible. Willpower is a joke. And yet the person doesn't look particularly different on the outside. There is no cast or bandage to see." Mike, Ellen, and Sue were nodding. "Sometimes you can't point to a cause or any specific problem. 'So why can't mom or dad or sister or whomever just get out and get going?' You can't imagine how many times I've been asked that question and how hard it is to explain."

Mike spoke up. "I totally agree. I'm always on the go—always able to carry on, usually creative at my work—then—and it's happened twice—it's almost like I'm completely different. During those times when I've been depressed I just didn't want to do anything; I became so tired I couldn't even think clearly; sometimes if I didn't know that I really felt like that I couldn't imagine it happening."

Ellen turned to Mike. "I had no idea . . ."

"Well, it's been a while and I've been fine and it's not something I have any reason to talk about." Mike paused. "Maybe like you didn't talk about your experience."

Ellen smiled. What Mike said was absolutely true. He smiled back. The mood in the room relaxed even more.

I was appreciative that Mike and Ellen were being so open. "Mike, would you mind a few more questions?"

"No."

"Did anything happen that in some way set off either of the two depressions?"

"You mean like some sort of stress?"

"Yes, Ellen became depressed following the birth of her child, and pregnancy can be stressful both physiologically and psychologically. I was wondering if anything specific happened that might have served as some sort of trigger for your depressions?"

"Well, the first time I became significantly depressed was about twelve years ago when I was twenty-four. I was working in New Jersey at the time and was dating somebody seriously. I had a job offer in Rutland, Vermont, and I wanted to move but she didn't. She didn't want to come even if we got married. I was crushed. I decided not to make the move at that time, but we broke up anyway. It was during that time that I started to go down—quickly. So I guess that depression was triggered by that experience."

"What about the second time?"

"That was different. It was three years later and I was still in New Jersey. Actually everything was great. I liked my job, had a new lady, didn't have any problems—and then bang, like a lead weight dropped on me."

"So there seemed to be no reason whatsoever?"

"No."

I looked toward Ellen. "Do you mind if I ask you a few questions?"

"That's okay." She seemed comfortable.

"Were there any other times when you went through a depression beside that postpartum episode?"

"I think I've had a tendency to get depressed about as long as I can remember, but it's never been as bad as the time after Julie was born."

"Do you ever have trouble premenstrually?"

"Yes, as a matter of fact. It's not always the same but some months about a week or so before my period I struggle—same stuff—no energy, irritable, I feel fuzzy-headed and very down, but then I know it won't last and I do what I can to get through it—better diet, more exercise, vitamins, and whatever else seems to help—and it has been a little better."

I glanced around the room. There were no yawns and no restless movements. Ellen looked like she was about to go on when Jean Brooks spoke up. I didn't know Jean's background. As a nursing supervisor she seemed to be comfortable and usually in control, an easy leader, well liked and respected.

"I don't think I've ever felt like Ellen or Mike described. I guess I've been down and upset about things, but I just keep going. Is it possible that I might someday become more seriously depressed?"

"I really don't know, Jean, but if you want me to guess I would say probably not."

"Why?"

"Because I think that depression has a lot in common with other medical illnesses."

"You mean psychological illnesses?"

"No, I mean medical illnesses."

Sue Lavender caught my eye with a knowing look. She had come to me as a patient, something that I wouldn't mention unless she brought it up. We had spent hours discussing her difficulties—the moods, the lack of energy that made it hard to focus on nursing or on being the best mother she could be to her eight-year-old daughter Jennifer. She already understood what I was about to say.

I continued my conversation with Jean. "Do you have children?"

"Yes."

"How many?"

"Three."

"Would you say that each child is quite different, quite individual, that each has a certain way of dealing with things that has been pretty consistent from the time they were infants?"

"Yes." She didn't hesitate.

"I've asked that question of parents for years and have almost always gotten the same response—in fact some mothers have pointed out that even in the womb one child was quiet and the other never stopped moving—and it continued true to form after they were born. It has seemed to me more and more clear that we're all brought into this world with a certain temperament, a certain energy level, a way of being. The longer I have been in this profession the more I have come to believe that this temperament or whatever you want to call it—this temperament that we all are born with—is just as physical as blue eyes or brown eyes or tallness or shortness. It's just there. As parents we profoundly influence our children. We try to do the best we can, but if one child is gold, one is steel, and one is fine china, you'll have a hell of a time trying to change that."

Jean was nodding her head. "So some of us are more prone to moodiness or whatever than others, and it's sort of built in?"

"Exactly. That's exactly what I mean. There is a very physical aspect to our emotions. That way we have of existing, that quality of self that each of us brings to the world is somehow there from the start. Of course what happens to us as children or anywhere along the path of life is profoundly important, but we are not blank screens. Just as important as our experiences, maybe even more important, is who we are in a temperamental sense."

I looked around the room. Everyone was quiet and looked thoughtful. I decided to continue, to explain in more detail. Understanding that this illness that had engulfed Michele, sweeping her into a living hell, was substantially medical as opposed to psychological somehow softened the anger that I felt that first night. It allowed me to be more objective—more professional. Maybe others in this room might feel the same way. It was worth a try.

I scanned the group. Everyone was thoughtful and quiet. I continued.

"What if you wanted to become a diabetic?" My eyebrows went up as I waited for a response. There were a few quizzical expressions. No one answered. I repeated the question. "Really— what if you wanted to develop diabetes?"

Elise said, "I'm not sure what you mean."

"Well, I know it's an odd way of looking at things, no one really wants diabetes, but what if you did? Do you think you could develop the illness?"

As I looked around the room at that moment there were a lot of thinking-hard expressions. A few people had sort of half smiles as though they were not quite sure if I was serious. There were a few shrugs.

"Let me explain. Every one of us is dealt a giant genetic deck

f cards. We have absolutely no control over the hand we've
een dealt.

"For each of us there are illnesses that we're almost incapable
f developing. For instance, probably some of us in this room
re not capable of developing diabetes no matter what we eat,
o matter how much sugar we take in, no matter how much
veight we gain, no matter how much stress we're under. Our
ancreatic chemistry is such that we will almost certainly main-
ain the capacity to regulate sugar in our bloodstream. Does that
nake sense?" Now heads began to nod. "Even if you wanted
liabetes you couldn't get it. There also may be those of us who are
ot capable of developing ulcers no matter what, or rheumatoid
rthritis, or coronary artery disease. Some people could probably
at all the fat and cholesterol they wanted and never develop
eart disease. Others can hardly control cholesterol even if they
at only carrots."

Mike interrupted, "I just read an article called 'The Prime
Minister and the Tennis Player.' It talked about Winston
Churchill, who had terrible health habit—he smoked constantly,
drank heavily, overate, and rarely exercised—and lived well into
is nineties without any evidence of heart disease. On the other
and Arthur Ashe, the professional tennis player, didn't smoke,
stayed trim, and seemed to lead a healthy life, yet he had two
eart attacks before he was forty. The article said it had a lot to
o with genetics. Essentially, about ten percent of the people are
almost immune from heart disease, and probably Churchill was
n that group—and about ten percent are very susceptible, like
Arthur Ashe. Probably, most of us fall somewhere in the middle."

I was nodding. "That is exactly what I'm talking about, and
or many illnesses, if not for most, the issue of genetic vulnerabil-
ty will be recognized as being more and more important. This
s why some of us might be more susceptible to the illnesses
that I mentioned, or to cancer or AIDS or even to the common
cold. And it's absolutely inconceivable that the same is not true

for emotional illness. Until recently we've considered the mind and emotion to be somehow different, as though it was somehow detached from the body, and that's not the way it works.

"We may think of the brain as a computer, but you can also think of it as a drug manufacturing company—producing more than two hundred drugs—prescribing them all the time to regulate so many things, your breathing, your temperature, your movement, your metabolism. And it has the huge job of regulating your interaction with your environment—with other people. There are probably a dozen or more of these brain drugs constantly working to manage your affect, your mood, anxiety, temperament—whatever. And to think that we are all the same in this way is not realistic. Some of us run faster, jump higher, play the piano better, do math easier, are more artistic, and on and on. So temperamentally—affectively—we're just as different. Already a number of genes have been identified that play a part in mood, temperament, or even the perception of reality."

I looked toward Jean Brooks again. "So when you asked me if you might some day become very depressed and I said no, I was just guessing, but it's an educated guess. I'm assuming that you've not had a significant depression so far in your life. I know nothing about your family, but if there seems to be little evidence of emotional difficulty, then I suspect that you'll be okay. Perhaps with enough stress you could be pushed into a major depression—I just don't know, but I doubt that you are at high risk."

Mike spoke up immediately. "So Ellen and I were born more vulnerable—that's what you are saying?"

"I think so."

Mike looked a little bleak. "I'm not sure how that makes me feel."

"Do you think you'd feel differently if instead of vulnerability to mood problems you were more vulnerable to blood pressure control problems, or ulcer disease, or arthritis, or diabetes, or whatever?"

"Probably."

"Well, that's honest—and I think many people feel that way. Somehow it's okay if it's 'physical.' If you can't control your sugar or your blood pressure it's okay, but having mood problems is a sign of weakness. If you have diabetes you have chemical imbalance in the pancreas. If you have arthritis, especially certain kinds, you have chemical imbalance in the immune system. If you have ulcer disease you have chemical imbalance in the stomach. Imbalance in the chemistry involved with fat metabolism predisposes to coronary artery disease. So, does it make sense that if you have difficulty with mood you might have a chemical imbalance in parts of the brain?"

There was a very short silence and then Mike looked up again. "Wait a minute. If chemistry is so important, when does psychology come into this? You asked me about stress."

"Psychological stress is important." I looked around—"How many of you blush?" Most hands went up. "Well, you don't blush because someone physically touched you—no one pinched your nose—you blush because you have a strong emotion and that feeling is instantly translated into a chemical change that increases the circulation in your face. So we're constantly 'blushing' inside, all the time—constantly adjusting our internal chemistry. And psychological stress can be part of the equation. It can bring out medical problems—but"—I paused and spoke to Mike—"Your particular vulnerability is crucial—and I'm not talking just to you, Mike, I'm talking to all of us. If your vulnerability is to gastric imbalance you may develop ulcers; if your vulnerability is to brain imbalance you may become seriously depressed."

I looked at everyone. "You know it may seem disheartening to think that you are vulnerable to a particular problem, but we all have some vulnerability. Actually it's really helpful to know and to be clear what that vulnerability is. It is in your best interest to do what you can to minimize the specific circumstances that may cause you problems but may not cause somebody else problems. By the same token there are probably many illnesses that each of us will never have to worry about. Put your efforts where they count the most. That's really intelligent preventive medicine."

I realized that we had drifted away from a discussion about Michele's situation, but this was so important and everyone seemed to be genuinely interested. I continued. "When it comes to preventing depression there are ways that anyone might be able to reduce their risk. If circumstances at home or work are particularly stressful, you can sometimes make changes. Long standing troubling issues that reflect childhood problems may act like a burr under the saddle, constantly gnawing, constantly working against you even if you don't really know it. If that is the case, by all means deal with it. This is the sort of situation where therapy may be very helpful. Or if there are physical circumstances that are stressful, like rapid hormonal changes such as those that occur premenstrually or in the postpartum, there may be ways you can improve your situation. Sometimes in these situations attention to nutrition and exercise and things of that nature are just not enough. Sometimes medications are a real advantage because we are dealing with a physical condition, one that may well be made worse by some sort of psychological stress or hormonal stress, but still a physical condition."

I looked around the room again. Again it was Mike who broke the silence. "Well, actually, I wanted to ask you about that too. You are giving Michele desipramine. Now, when I was having my rough time I was given imipramine. They sound alike. Are they related?"

"Yes, they're both antidepressants and they are chemically related."

"I remember not really knowing what the medication was doing—well, maybe I slept a little better. I took it for a few months and when I stopped taking it everything seemed okay without it so I was never really sure whether it helped or not."

"Mike, these medications are very misunderstood. Did your physician explain very much at the time you began to take the medication?"

"I'm not sure but I don't really think so."

I looked around the room. "Is everyone interested in this, or should I talk with Mike after we're done?"

"No, go ahead." Jean Brooks spoke without taking a poll, but other heads were nodding.

"Mike, did your doctor suggest that you stop the imipramine when you did?"

"Not really, I just sort of let it run out."

"Why?"

"Well, I was feeling okay and I didn't think it was doing very much."

"Anything else?"

"What do you mean?"

"Well, let's say that the medication you were taking was for high blood pressure instead of low mood, do you think you would have let it run out?"

Mike raised his eyebrows and a faint smile crossed his face. "Probably not."

"So why do you think it was okay to let this run out?"

"Well, actually, I always felt a little uncomfortable taking it."

"You mean it made you sick?"

"No—I just felt—I don't know, like somehow it was a crutch. Like I shouldn't need it." He paused for a second, "And I think I was always a little afraid of getting hooked on the medication."

"Did you ever ask your doctor about this?"

Mike sort of closed one eye and furrowed his brow as if he were scanning his memory—"I don't think I did."

"Well, I don't know if this fits for you, Mike, but a lot of people feel almost guilty about taking antidepressants, as if somehow they have a character flaw if they have to take something like this."

"Well, that sounds right," Mike said, "I felt that way. In fact that's exactly why I stopped taking it."

"You know it's interesting—if someone has a chemical imbalance in the pancreas and they have diabetes, they usually accept insulin or other medication to correct it. If someone has a chemical imbalance in the kidney or the vascular system and their blood pressure is too high, they accept medication to regulate it. But if someone has a chemical imbalance in the brain that leads to mood problems or anxiety, as soon as medication works many people want to stop it—'it's a crutch.'"

Mike had a sheepish smile on his face. I thought he was about to say something but Mary Bragdon spoke first. "Don't antidepressants stimulate you in some way—sort of get you high?"

Mary had been very quiet for a long time, and I think of all the people in the room she had been the most upset when we started. Now she did seem more relaxed. I deflected her question to Mike. "Did you ever feel high when you were taking the imipramine?"

"No, not really," Mike answered, "I sort of felt okay—more like my old self."

I turned to Mary. "On the streets of New York City you could find any stimulant or tranquilizer you wanted—but you probably wouldn't find imipramine or desipramine or other antidepressants because they don't give you any sort of buzz or fuzz. In fact, it often takes a few weeks before they begin to work, and when they do it is sometimes so subtle that you may not be sure it's the medication that is helping. It's like Mike said, you just feel like your old self before the depression, you feel like you would feel normally when you are feeling good, not altered."

"So it's not a tranquilizer or a stimulant?" Jean Brooks seemed very curious.

"No, Jean, and it's not addicting either.—Let's go back to New York City. If I were to stand on a street corner there and give a hundred people Valium . . ."

Liz Gold broke in without missing a beat. "You would probably be a hero." There were a few outright chuckles and everyone was smiling.

"That's probably true—anyway, almost every one of those hundred people would react in a similar fashion—that is they would feel mellow or tranquilized—not normal. But with an antidepressant—it's like Mike said, you just feel like your old self before the depression. These medications are normalizing, not abnormalizing."

"If I took the medication would it help me feel better?" It was Jean Brooks again.

"That's an interesting question, Jean—again I can't be sure but I doubt it would help."

"Why not?"

"First of all, unless someone is truly depressed in a chemical way it is likely that they would not benefit from this sort of medication. In that same group of a hundred people who I tried to give medication to, only some, maybe twenty percent, would be biochemically depressed at any given time. Even then, only some members of that group would respond to any particular medication because we are all chemically unique, different physically, and the way that depression occurs in terms of these brain chemicals is undoubtedly not the same for everyone. So out of a hundred people, almost a hundred might respond to Valium, while only twenty or so would benefit from antidepressant medications in general. And of the twenty who would benefit from some antidepressant medication, maybe half would chemically fit with a specific antidepressant. Mike seemed to be helped by imipramine, but the next person might have no response whatsoever. So in your case, Jean, I doubt that in general these medications would help."

Ellen Goldman had been listening intently. "When Michele was in intensive care it seemed to me that she was withdrawn, quiet—I guess depressed, but it didn't really seem dramatic. I figured she was probably worse before the shooting, which didn't make sense except that I thought that the medication was helping her. But from what you're saying it may have been too soon for it to work. Is that right?"

"To tell you the truth, I have no idea. Sometimes someone does seem to respond more quickly, but often it does take weeks. And I agree with you, Ellen, I know what you mean about Michele. Both her mother and Jeff told me that the way she was depressed before the shooting somehow seemed different. I actually doubt it is the medication that has made the difference—I really don't have a good explanation."

Sue Lavender said, "I thought shrinks are supposed to understand everything." She was smiling. I smiled back. "Bull." Everyone smiled.

# 28

Friday, April 17, was gorgeous. The sky was bright blue with a few wispy clouds, humidity was low, and the temperature was in the mid-seventies, unusually high. Michele was in my office for her first appointment.

She sat directly across from me looking somewhat sheepish as the barking continued from the front yard. I stood up from my chair and walked to the open window. The barking drew my gaze down where I could see a very plump white, brown, and black dog tied to a tree, frantically trying to break loose. It was Old Milwaukee, the dog Jeff bought for Michele once upon a time, in a different lifetime.

Since Michele had come home from the hospital she and Millie had been inseparable; man's best friend was always loyal and affectionate and never asked difficult questions. Michele took "the beast" everywhere.

"I'm sorry," she said, "but it was sort of warm and I didn't want to keep Millie closed in the stuffy car—but I didn't think she would keep up this racket."

"Why don't you bring her inside?"

That was probably the first time I saw Michele smile. Millie never again missed a session.

Perhaps it was the comfort that Michele felt with her trusted pet in the room, or maybe it was just time. As she stood up to leave a few minutes later, as our time was ending, she turned and withdrew a letter from her pocketbook. It was written to one of her closest friends in New Jersey, and she had already decided that it couldn't be mailed. She said, "I'd like you to read this. We can talk about it later." Sometimes people deliver the most important messages at the end of an hour.

The door quietly closed and I sat down in my chair. By the time I finished the letter I had goose bumps and moist eyes. The curtain had just begun to open.

*April 16, 1987*

    *Dear Lynn,*

    *I feel a need to write to you now. Carol sent me a note because she hadn't heard from me and was worried. She asked about Josh and I just lost control. I said to Jeff, "How can I tell Carol and Lynn? How in the Hell can I ever tell them?"*

    *Jeff said you had called and he had already told you. How shocked you must have been.*

    *For a while I didn't know what happened. When I woke up in the hospital following surgery I didn't know why I was there. Jeff told me gradually. When he said that I shot myself— and then I asked about the baby—his face went white. All he said was, "Josh is no longer with us."*

    *It didn't take much to put two and two together. God, how I wanted to die. I still do. Every time I think of him I wish I were dead. I tried to commit suicide twice and I'm still here. Why?*

    *I figure this is my punishment. How can I ever live with myself? Nothing will ever be the same. I have not felt like seeing anyone or talking to anyone. It feels odd to have people being kind to me. Everyone should hate me for what I have done. I do.*

    *For the past two years all I've wanted was to give Jeff a child.*

Especially a son. I felt I was mature enough to handle the responsibility. I felt we would be good parents.

Despite the trauma of Joshua's birth, I felt our lives were blessed. I believed that he survived because he was to be special and enrich our lives more than most people—and now it's all gone. Jeff was so proud. He was so good with him and he helped me a great deal. But no one saw the intensity of my depression. I did at times, but I kept fighting it, saying to myself that I would get through this thing. I always did with PMS, even when I felt my whole self caving in—I would get through it. So every time I looked at Josh, I said to myself, "Remember how much you wanted him—although it seems like you will feel this lousy forever, it'll get better." Well, it never did.

Lynn, something happened that I lost control of. It was like a demon or something, because I still can't picture myself with the gun. I've always been afraid of them.

They tried to tell me that many women go through this postpartum thing, so why did I have to be so extreme, so different? And to do what I did—I can't remember doing it. I don't think I ever want to remember.

I can't understand how Jeff can even look at me. I have taken something from him that can never be replaced. All I know is—my beautiful baby is dead and I am responsible. This is something I can never get a grip on. After all the waiting, the planning, the anticipation, the money we spent buying things for him—all our dreams have been shattered.

Why me? I keep asking myself, why me? And why was I spared when I so desperately wanted to die? I should have died. I have no right to be here. I don't know what happens from here. I can't think past today.

I see Dr. Burak, a psychiatrist, and feel comfortable with him, but I'm not sure talking about it helps or ever will help. How can anyone expect me to live with it? Could you?

I know you're thinking of me and I thank you for caring. It might be a while between letters. I know you're crying. I've been

*crying through every word I write. I wake up crying every
night. I don't foresee any end to the tears. I see his precious face
everywhere and I can't stand myself. I am sorry for upsetting
you, but I feel I should write you at least this once—*

*Take care my friend,*

MICHELE

# 29

Even before Michele was out of surgery a surprising number of people knew what was happening. At any time, day or night, including Saturday night, many Benningtonians are tuned constantly to gossip central—their CB scanners. As the police and rescue calls went out, the community's phone lines blazed. In a town where the opening of a new restaurant is major news, the murder/attempted suicide on April 4 was lightning striking parched grass.

For those who hadn't heard by Sunday morning, the local radio stations WHGC and WBTN repeated the story ad nauseam. Monday's front page article in the Bennington *Banner* was anticlimactic. Under the bleak front-page picture of the Remington home on Jefferson Street was an inch-high headline stating BABY KILLED. The story was cautiously written:

A six week old baby was killed and his mother was hospitalized from gunshot wounds they suffered in their home on Saturday evening, Police Chief Howard Safe said.

Joshua Remington died at South-Western Vermont Medical Center on Saturday while his mother, Michele Remington, was listed in serious but stable condition on Sunday, Safe said.

He said no arrests had been made by Sunday afternoon, and that police were still trying to piece together how the shooting occurred.

On Tuesday April 7, the *Banner*'s story about the shooting was still low-key:

Bennington police pieced together parts of a puzzle Monday, trying to understand the tragic and unprecedented shooting of a baby and his mother Saturday.

Police have yet to determine exactly what happened in the apartment at 112 Jefferson on Saturday evening but say they have theories. However, they declined to speculate until they are sure.

By Tuesday there was probably not one person in Bennington County who didn't know, or hadn't heard, that Michele was the "killer." The animosity and anger toward this "bitch" was palpable. She should fry.

Richard Kelley, the always aggressive Bennington County state's attorney, was perched like a surfer riding a tidal wave of community emotion. Lengthy investigative reports supported his decision to charge Michele with murder in the first degree.

John Henry was well liked. His father had been a tailor in Bennington for many years. Like his father, John was hardworking and reliable, but he had not followed in his father's footsteps. Much to the satisfaction of the elder Henry, his son had become a lawyer. A physically big man, at fifty-one John was overweight and bellyish.

In the first moments of crisis in the emergency department Jeff Remington felt as though he were drowning. Although everyone was solicitous, the questions kept coming. All Jeff could think of at that moment was that he needed a lawyer—right away. It was natural that he would turn to John Henry. He had known John Henry for as long as he had memory. John had been his dad's attorney and had always been someone the family could trust. Fortunately for Jeff, when he called the Henrys' home number that night, John was there. He arrived at the hospital ten minutes after receiving the call.

Like many small-town attorneys, John Henry was a jack-of-all-trades. One person through the door wanted a divorce, the next a will, the next a partnership agreement. And always someone needed defending because of driving while intoxicated. However, he had never defended anyone charged with murder and in his heart of hearts he did not look forward to this prospect.

A week later, when his secretary informed him that the state's attorney was on the line, he felt a tinge of discomfort. John had spoken to Richard Kelley literally hundreds of times. On this occasion Kelley's voice was somehow quieter. "John, I've held off indicting Mrs. Remington while she's been in the hospital, but I'd like to get this done as soon as she is out. Perhaps it would be easier in your office.

A few minutes later John Henry buzzed his secretary, "Loretta, will you get Jeff Remington on the line." It seemed almost immediately that his secretary buzzed back, "Jeff's on the line, Mr. Henry."

"Hi, Jeff, it's John—how're you doing?"

"Just fair, trying to hang in there, what's up?"

"Well, there is some business related to Michele's charges that have to be taken care of and I was wondering how soon she might be leaving the hospital."

"It looks like it could be tomorrow, John—why?"

"Well, could you bring her to my office on your way home?"

"Let me see how she's feeling—okay? Why don't I call you in the morning and let you know."

Tuesday, April 14, dawned brightly. Spring was finally sniffable. Had I known that Michele was going to be charged with murder immediately after stepping foot out of the hospital I would have been very upset. I couldn't put off the inevitable, but I would have preferred that this legal confrontation occur while she was still in the hospital where experienced personnel would be available if the shock of a first-degree murder charge penetrated the shell of numbness and amnesia that had been protecting her. But I didn't know, and Jeff was there at ten-thirty in the morning to get her.

Michele also knew nothing of the visit to John Henry's office until she was actually walking out of the hospital. She didn't object, however, because she wasn't really capable of objecting to very much at this point.

At one time Henry's office had been a private residence on Maple Street. The house was white clapboard with black shutters, and on the front lawn, appropriately enough, stood two handsome maples.

Loretta Smith, Henry's longtime secretary, had known Michele's parents for a number of years. Somehow she had never met Michele, but the whole tragic affair had taken on a very personal tone. She was nervous in anticipation of the couple's arrival. But she didn't act nervous at eleven o'clock when the door opened and Michele and Jeff entered. "Good morning, why don't you both take a seat for a moment and I'll call Mr. Henry." She picked up the phone and buzzed her boss.

John opened the door to his office and greeted the couple warmly. This was the first time he had seen Michele since the shooting; she appeared pale and tired. In fact they both looked horrible, just what you would expect after what they had been through. John spoke softly. "Could you both come in the office for a few minutes, we need to talk." Michele stood up and walked past Henry into his office. Jeff followed. Once a living room, the spacious work area was comfortably appointed with a large carved antique desk, leather chairs, a large antique wall map of old Bennington, a number of tasteful prints and a few diplomas. The fireplace, often in use in the winter months, contained a vase of spring flowers that greatly brightened the room. One of the two maroon leather chairs in front of John's desk was at that moment warmed by the rays of the sun streaming through a southeast window. Michele chose to sit in the other chair.

After inquiring about her health, John came right to the point. There was no easy way to say what he had to say. "Michele, in a few minutes Detective Bowers is going to be here with some papers for you to sign. Because of what's happened you're being charged with the murder of your son Joshua."

Michele looked down at the floor but her expression hardly changed. No, she didn't have any questions.

As John watched Michele looking so tired and sad, he felt a wave of compassion. Deep down he was confused about what had happened. He didn't understand how this quiet young woman could possibly have done what she did. Jim Bowers, the chief detective on the case, mentioned that she probably had postpartum depression, about which John knew little. He was not very experienced with the insanity defense, but there seemed to be no better route to take if he was going to protect his client.

There was some noise in the outer office. John got up and opened his door. Jim Bowers had arrived and he was immediately invited in.

According to Jeff the brief meeting was almost eerie. Everyone was quiet. Michele continued to show little emotion.

After she had been officially charged Jeff put his arm about his wife's shoulder. "Let's go, honey." Jim Bowers and John Henry glanced at each other. Jeff didn't notice. Nodding to both men he sort of lifted Michele out of the chair, gently guiding her to the outer office.

John's voice was quiet as he spoke, "Jeff, could you come back in for a moment?"

"I'll be right back, honey—wait here." Michele sat dutifully like a puppet.

"What is it, John?"

"Jeff, I need to know something—how much money could you put up if we needed something for Michele's bail?"

Jeff was shaken. Had Michele not been injured on April 4, she probably would have gone to jail—at least for a little while. But somehow he had denied the possibility that it could still happen. His voice almost quivered. "We have very little, actually nothing except the property where we've started to build. Maybe we could borrow against it or even sell it—but that's it."

John Henry glanced again at Jim Bowers, then he said, "Jeff, take Michele home and wait for my call. I'll see what I can arrange."

All afternoon Michele did not speak unless it was in response to a question. Jeff watched her sitting in her rocker, moving slowly to and fro. "Maybe she shouldn't be at home," he thought. "If she has to go to jail she'd be better off in the hospital."

At three-thirty in the afternoon the phone's ring broke the silence. Overall Jeff was relieved when he heard what John had to say. Judge William Myers released Michele on her own recognizance as long as she met certain conditions; only the last condition bothered him.

(1) The defendant shall personally appear in court as required by notice to the defendant or the defendant's attorney, or be in violation of this order.

(2) Defendant shall let his/her attorney or the court clerk know where s/he is at all times, and a telephone number and address where s/he may be reached.

(3) Defendant shall not be charged with, and have probable cause for, a felony, a crime against the person, or an offense like the offense s/he is now charged with.

(4) Defendant shall report to the Bennington Police Department in person one day per week.

(5) Defendant shall reside in Bennington County and shall not travel outside of that county without written permission from this Court.

(6) Defendant shall not purchase, possess, or use any firearms.

(7) Parties request DEFENDANT be examined for competency and insanity pursuant to 13VSA 4814 (a) 1 & 2.

# 30

The Bennington Monument commemorates a pivotal American Revolutionary battle that actually took place nine miles west of Bennington in what is now New York State. Surprisingly like the Washington Monument, this massive granite obelisk dominates the town's nonskyline, standing proudly out of place amidst the low mountains of southern Vermont. Dr. James Timmons lives in one of the very elegant homes surrounding the monument.

Dr. Timmons is sometimes called upon by the Bennington courts for psychiatric evaluations. In the 1950s and '60s and even into the '70s, Dr. Timmons was a very busy man. He found time to guide the local counseling service, work in the hospital, maintain a private practice, publish papers on the care of emotionally disturbed children, and lecture widely. Less active now, he continues to see some patients in his home and some in a second office in nearby Williamstown.

Michele was ordered to see Dr. Timmons twice, on April 20 and 29. He was asked to answer two questions: Was Michele competent to stand trial? Was she insane at the time of the shootings?

In the eyes of American law, a person must have the mind of a criminal, the intent to do the crime, and a true appreciation of what they are doing—otherwise what he or she does may be sad or tragic, but it is not considered criminal. According to our law, one must always look at the circumstances and not just the act itself in determining whether someone is guilty or innocent. Insanity is not the only circumstance that may be considered.

Suppose for instance that a child darts into the street and a driver has absolutely no chance to stop in time. The child is killed. A crime? Absolutely not. Suppose, however, that the driver has a history of epilepsy—that he has had seizures in the past, but none for many years. Suppose further that he is taking appropriate medications and has not missed any doses and that he has a valid driver's license. Then, tragically and unexpectedly there is a "breakthrough seizure" while he is at the wheel and his car jumps a curb and kills a pedestrian. A crime? According to our laws it shouldn't be. There was no negligence, awareness, ability to stop, or criminal intent.

These examples are reasonably easy. Much more difficult for most of us is the idea that mental illness or distorted thinking could also be used as evidence that someone did not have the appropriate "mens rea," the necessary criminal mind.

Insanity as a defense often seems hard to swallow. It is not a common experience that everyone understands. "What is it? Is it real? How could someone not know?" Michele Remington picked up a gun and shot twice. Did she understand what she was doing or didn't she? In the exact words of Vermont law:

A person is not responsible for criminal conduct if at the time of such conduct as a result of mental disease or defect he lacks adequate capacity to either appreciate the criminality of his conduct or to conform his conduct to the requirements of law.

The terms "mental disease or defect" do not include an abnormality manifested only by repeated criminal or what are otherwise anti-social conduct. The terms "mental disease or defect" shall include congenital and traumatic mental conditions as well as disease.

The defendant shall have the burden of proof in establishing insanity as an affirmative defense by a preponderance of the evidence.

On the evening before her second appointment with Dr. Timmons, Michele was scheduled to see me at 5:00 P.M. She and Millie were on time and I invited them into my office. My first glance at Michele told me there was something wrong. The aura of unhappiness that always surrounded Michele in those early days was heavier that evening. But as I watched her I also realized she was in physical pain. As she breathed she would suddenly catch herself, wince, sometimes hunch forward slightly.

"What's wrong?"

"Dr. Loy says I have an inflammation of the lining of the lung where the bullet did the damage."

"Pleurisy?"

"Yes, that's it. I'm taking medication—an antibiotic and . . ." she winced again and stopped in midsentence, "some aspirin—but it still hurts."

"Did Dr. Loy suggest going back into the hospital?"

"He said I might have to go if it gets worse, but there is no way I want to do that."

"Well, if you are too uncomfortable let me know, we could stop anytime and reschedule in a day or two."

"No—I want to talk."

For a few moments Michele seemed preoccupied and was silent. I waited.

"I know Jeff means well, but I can hardly move without him asking me if I'm okay. And he's always watching. I know he's afraid, but I'm not going to do anything to myself. I tried with pills and even with the gun and who knows how I would mess it up if I tried again."

This was not an entirely reassuring statement. "You've been thinking about it some?"

"I guess so." She glanced up and probably saw concern in my

face—"Oh, no, I'm not thinking of doing anything, it's just that I've been feeling upset and it's not about anything specific, it's just a feeling."

Jeff Remington had called earlier in the week. He had accompanied Michele to Dr. Timmons's appointment, and he thought Michele was "different" in the days that followed, more irritable, perhaps a little sadder. "Had she said much about the meeting afterwards?"

"No," Jeff said, "not a word."

After a few more seconds Michele spoke again. "Sometimes when I take a breath it hurts and it's like a knife in my chest and I want the pain to go away, yet it's also somehow okay that I'm feeling it."

Crime and punishment. It was okay to feel a knife of pain because she deserved it, that was the implication. I looked at Michele and was struck with a feeling of sadness that made me swallow hard. The enormity of what she had done washed over me again. The pain of pleurisy would succumb to time and medication, but the hole in her life that she had created with her actions would live forever in her soul. There would be times of ease, of vagueness, of almost forgetting—but there would also be moments of remembering, possibly with increasing clarity—lifelong punctuation marks of anguish.

Perhaps Millie sensed the moment because she suddenly roused herself and ambled over to her mistress. Placing her head on Michele's knee she gazed at her with eyes that to me seemed even sadder and more forlorn than usual. Michele scratched absentmindedly behind Millie's ears. "It's a good thing I didn't bring Millie to see Dr. Timmons last week. Did you know that he sees patients with his own dogs in the office?" A few other patients who had seen Jim Timmons mentioned the dogs, two giant Newfoundlands who stood guard over their master. I imagined this could be intimidating to some patients, but I think the dogs put Michele at ease.

"Yes, I've heard about that. But aside from the dogs, how did the meeting go?"

"I guess it went okay," Michele said. "Jeff was with me and he asked both of us a lot of questions—no real surprises."

"I suspect it wasn't easy talking about Josh?" I rarely mentioned Josh's name to Michele. She looked at me and turned her head in such a way that for an instant there was no reflection on the surface of her glasses and I could see her eyes. For a brief moment, maybe for the first time, I could see the pain.

"What I'm really afraid of is the meeting tomorrow," she continued. "Dr. Timmons asked me to bring both Jeff and my mother. I always feel the tension between them and right now I don't know if I can take it if they start to argue."

I thought this unlikely, but I didn't say anything. In the aftermath of tragedy Jeff Remington and Helen Cort had called a truce. It might be temporary, but for the moment they were both feeling very much in need of mutual support; they were both riding in the same tragic boat. Michele spoke again. "But even more than mom and Jeff getting in to it, I'm afraid that mom will hear that I was upset with her for being so intense in those last few weeks of my pregnancy, and so pushy and outrageous when the baby came home. I'm not blaming her, but I'm afraid that if I explain all the circumstances to Dr. Timmons she will take it the wrong way. She is just so touchy and sensitive that I know she will feel deeply hurt and that's not what I want."

I didn't try to minimize Michele's concern. Helen had already made a few comments to me that suggested that she was struggling with some of the things that had happened. Unfortunately, protecting Helen or Jeff or anyone else from a backlash of guilt took second place to caring for Michele. I looked at her there, sitting across from me, stroking Millie's head. In deflecting concern from herself to others she was still keeping some of her own feelings at bay. But deep down, or maybe not so deep down, she knew as I knew that the meetings with Dr. Timmons were crucial. Legally she was fighting for her life. First-degree murder is the most serious accusation in the world of criminal law. Dr. Timmons was the first outside expert to pronounce whether or not he felt that Michele really was a criminal or a victim herself.

# 31 🍂

While I was in San Francisco training to be a psychiatrist, an article appeared in the *Chronicle* entitled "Two Hundred and Seventeen Therapies Available in the Bay Area!" Freudian psychoanalysts were free-associating; primal screamers required sound engineers; cognitive therapists restructured errant thought patterns; behaviorists dealt in rewards and punishments; and Jungians pursued the collective unconscious, those mysterious and sometimes mystical common threads that seemed to bind the fabric of humanity. All of these approaches have value and at one time or another every one helps. But there are no formulas.

Whatever approach is taken, what seems to be most important is the development of a relationship involving mutual trust and respect between patient and therapist. That is why Michele's legal situation continued to bother me.

Even though my conviction that Michele was no criminal grew stronger with each meeting; even though I believed with all my heart that she was no criminal, that she had acted as a result of confused, distorted, and delusional thinking, I could not entirely cast aside that haunting personal doubt. Under the circumstances could I really be objective?

My discomfort grew even more as I found my legal background seeping through in other ways. Michele or Jeff would tell me what John Henry was doing and not doing and I began to wonder whether he was being sufficiently aggressive in preparing her defense. "Has Mr. Henry called you?" Michele would ask.

"Not yet."

"Oh—he said he was going to."

"I'm sure he will," I would say reassuringly.

I was torn. I did not want to focus on legal matters and confuse my role as Michele's therapist with that of an expert witness or legal advisor, but I was more and more certain that Michele was not guilty under the law and that she needed to be given this legal "dispensation" if at all possible. I realized that in an ironic way the pronouncement of a jury that she was not guilty, even if the cause were insanity, might be salve for her internal torture. If a jail sentence were to result from the pending legal battle, the incarceration itself would not be the real punishment. Rather, it would be the meaning of that sentence—that other people believed that Michele's actions were really intended, that she was truly the basest and most vile kind of human being, that she had taken the life of her own child consciously and with malice aforethought—that would be the condemnation that would kill Michele.

After Michele saw Jim Timmons for her evaluation, I continued to work in legal silence but I was insatiably curious about his report. Not only was it important strategically to Michele, it was important to me as a measure of my own objectivity. If Dr. Timmons agreed that Michele did not have the mens rea, the criminal mind, my haunting self-doubts would fade.

The report arrived in the mail in early June. It sat on my desk until the evening when I finished seeing patients. I had a number of phone calls to make, as usual, but I couldn't wait. I tore open the envelope and sat quietly for the next ten minutes reading.

When I finished I remember looking up and staring across the room at a painting. It was my favorite painting, and that's why it hung in my office even though it was out of place with the rest of the decor. It was Haitian, a fairly large and dramatic work of a dense banana-laden jungle. Like much of Haitian art, something about this painting was mysterious and impenetrable. Something about the way Dr. Timmons wrote his report was similar. I felt comfortable with what he had to say, yet I realized that he had not entirely closed the door to misunderstanding.

May 15, 1987

Dear Judge Myers,

I am writing with regard to Mrs. Michele Remington. Mrs. Remington was seen on 4/20 and 4/29/87. On both occasions she was driven to and from my office by her husband. On the second occasion she was also accompanied by her mother at my request. As already mentioned, she was aware of the nature and significance of the examination. She was neatly and cleanly dressed and exhibited good personal hygiene. She wore eyeglasses. She was somewhat overweight. Her speech was logical, coherent, and relevant but very sparse and underproductive. Her mood was clearly depressive. As already described, Mrs. Remington, except for PMS, had been an emotionally stable individual until the last trimester of her pregnancy. She clearly exhibited signs of significant weight gain, fluid retention, and depression during the last trimester of her pregnancy. She was forced to stop working. Her infant exhibited signs of asphyxia following delivery and was hospitalized at Albany Medical Center for twelve days. He was discharged with an uncertain prognosis as to CNS (brain damage). This was especially troubling to Mrs. Remington because of her brother's mental retardation following birth damage.

Following delivery Mrs. Remington clearly developed a severe postpartum depression as a result of which she was unable to adequately care for herself, infant, or husband. She was clearly not only depressed but felt guilty and responsible for her 'failures' and her infant's probable brain damage. She attempted suicide by overdose of medication shortly before the shooting incident. On 3/31/87 she was seen by Dr. Greer and presumably she stated to him that she was not certain she would not harm her infant.[1]

One 4/4/87 while her husband was outside the home she shot her infant and herself. Mrs. Remington does not describe any hallucinations[2] but showed signs of having a delusional belief that she was responsible for what went wrong in her infant prior to 4/4/87.

Based on all the evidence available to this examiner, at the time of the alleged incident Mrs. Remington was clearly suffering from a severe postpartum depression with psychotic features. *Although she was not overtly legally insane at the time of the alleged offense, this examiner does not believe she had the mental state required for the offense charged.*

A few days later, on May 18, Judge Myers asked Dr. Timmons to comment specifically on Michele's competency to stand trial.

May 22, 1987

Dear Judge Myers,

This is in response to your letter of 5/18/87 regarding Michele G. Remington's competency. As I stated in my letter of 5/14/87, I did not believe she was mentally responsible for the alleged offense because she did not 'have the mental state required for the offense charged.' When seen by me, Mrs. Remington was mentally competent to stand trial in as much as she understood the nature of the alleged offense, knew the consequences of the alleged offense, and was capable of assisting counsel in her own defense. She was also aware of the judicial process if she did have to go to trial. In all

---

[1]Whether or not Dr. Greer asked this question will never be known. His written notes of Michele's visit contain no mention of any statement about possibly harming the baby. Furthermore, upon questioning him directly, he told me that he does not remember asking that question.

[2]I too did not know about Michele's hallucinatory experiences at the time that the Timmons report first appeared. It was during Michele's therapy session some weeks later that she disclosed her upsetting debates with the faceless man, which she had experienced while at her parents' home in the week prior to the shooting.

fairness to Mrs. Remington, at the time I last saw her, namely 4/29/87, she was still severely depressed and under the active psychiatric care of Dr. Carl Burak. It is my professional opinion based on that last interview that if a trial were to occur at this time, it could pose a serious threat to her mental well-being.

I have no intention of seeing Mrs. Remington again, but I would be more than happy to do so if the Court desires same.

Yours truly,
JAMES M. TIMMONS, M. D.

# 32 🪶

In my office I have a favorite chair covered in wide-wale corduroy. I bought it in 1978 in San Francisco after graduating my residency program. As usual I sat there. Michele sat across from me on the small loveseat more recently purchased one snowy day in Brattleboro. I wrote the date on her chart, "May 22, 1987." Millie padded around the room, nudged my knee once, and settled down with a grunt next to my chair. Michele watched her absentmindedly and then reached into her pocketbook, withdrawing a small blue clothbound book, which she handed to me.

"What's this?" I was reluctant to open the book without her permission.

"It's a journal that Dr. Benjamin asked me to keep about my PMS problems. I would like you to read it."

"Dr. Benjamin?" For a moment the name didn't click.

"The obstetrician in Williamstown."

"Oh, yes," I said. I knew Dr. Benjamin by reputation (a good one) but we had never met.

"You had premenstrual problems?"

"Real bad. Dr. Benjamin asked me to change my diet, take some vitamins and primrose oil, and do some extra walking."

I opened the journal. The first entry jumped at me.

### WEDNESDAY, JANUARY 29, 1986

*Real depressed, energy level falling, wanted to be alone. Went to work at 7:00 A.M.—at 11:00 it hit like a ton of bricks. Couldn't bear it. Pain in right leg was horrible. Couldn't eat lunch, doubling over in chair. Should've gone out for a walk instead. Had to stand the remaining three hours, irritable to no end. Littlest things set me off. Felt like destroying something or even someone. Wanted to die.*

*Jeff knew, helped me through it this time, talked to me and was my shoulder. He's learning to deal with this thing but it is not enough, I don't want to go through it, I can't take much more of it. Only twenty-one days since last one.*

### FRIDAY, JANUARY 31

*Well, today was better as far as the pain, but had the "sluggos," which come after the pain. Anybody who can live through that would be worn out too. It just takes every ounce of energy from me because it's so difficult to do even normal things. Don't know how I made it through work, feel so depressed, so drained. Came home and fell asleep at 8:00 P.M., something I never do in front of the TV. I'm always on the go. This whole week has been a waste. Had two more accidents at work. Three out of five fingers are now injured.*

### MONDAY, FEBRUARY 24

*Started to get up for work, the clock got faster, I got slower, I'll never make it on time. It's that phase of time slipping from me again. I look in the mirror and feel thoroughly disgusted. God, I hate this, packed it in and went downstairs to the couch. That's where I stayed all day, the light was bothering me, any light. The living room is dark anyway so I just stayed there and watched movies all day. Jeff went up to his father's birthday, I stayed. This day was worthless . . .*

### TUESDAY, FEBRUARY 25

*Do feel somewhat better, my eyes don't hurt, but my headache is still there. I'm still so tired, where's my energy? It's like*

*something has sucked the life right out of me. Took Millie for a*
*ride to the carwash. Finally called Dr. Benjamin for another*
*appointment. Don't know what good it will do, I'm so tired of*
*trying new things and feeling that something is working and*
*then the next time I'm back to square one. I just can't take this*
*every month any more. It takes so much out of me, and then*
*forever to get back on my feet again. I wish I could give it away.*
*Feel like dying, but too much responsibility to commit*
*suicide. Ha. What a joke.*

I had goose bumps. I looked up, suddenly aware of Michele's
gaze. Tears were about to spill over her lower lids. "If you had
read what you are reading now before I had Joshua, would you
have warned me about postpartum depression?" She didn't wait
for an answer. "Somebody should've known, I should've known."
She began to cry. I reached for the always available Kleenex and
handed the box to her.

Michele's question was troubling. Through the years I'd seen
many women who were suffering with depression. In taking a
history I would often ask whether they had experienced postpartum depression. So many of the women had answered "Yes,"
but almost none had been referred for help during that time.
Now the picture had suddenly changed. In the seven weeks since
Michele's tragedy, I had received more postpartum referrals than
I had in the past seven years. It was as though the local medical
and psychological community had just awakened from a long
slumber. I felt like I had been sleeping too. Why hadn't any of
us been more tuned in?

Michele was blotting her eyes. I reached back and grabbed the
wastebasket, which was next to my desk, holding it out so she
could donate the tissues. No longer crying, she again looked at
me, waiting for my response.

"I'm not really sure that someone reading your journal ahead
of time would have connected the PMS with the possibility
of postpartum problems. Maybe they should have, but I'm not

159

certain. I'll try to find out." I paused for a moment, "There's a great deal we all have to learn."

Michele was quiet. "You can keep the journal for a while if it will help."

"Thanks." I rudely glanced down again unable to stop reading. The last few entries were different, suggesting that Dr. Benjamin's recommendations had begun to have an impact.

### WEDNESDAY, APRIL 16

*No sign of discomfort, a little back pain and headache, but cramps and bloating are gone. I can't believe it. Why can't this be like this every month? I can't believe even the first day wasn't too bad. I know it won't last, it would be a miracle if it did. But maybe the next month will be half as good.*

### SUNDAY, MAY 11

*Most cramps gone. Suffered headache all day, but other than that everything was fine. Can't believe it—wasn't too bad. My eyes hurt but that was probably from lack of sleep.*

At that point the journal abruptly ended. I made a quick calculation—there were no further entries because Michele had become pregnant with Joshua.

# 33 🍂

The intercom buzzed and I picked up. "Sorry," Linda said, "I didn't want to interrupt but Jeff Remington is on the line and he sounds very upset."

Terrible thoughts flashed through my mind. It was late June, Michele had been quietly trying to get through each day. I always wondered what would happen if her memory returned or if for any reason she experienced an avalanche of feeling that crushed her. Was this it? Had the shoe dropped?

"That's okay, Lin, I'm between patients." I pushed the blinking button.

"Hi, Jeff. What's happening?"

"Have you seen today's paper?"

"No."

"Let me read something to you," he said.

"Go ahead."

The headline says:

"REMINGTON WAS SANE/INFANTICIDE TRIAL POSSIBLE." Jeff continued, "Michele G. Remington, charged with killing her six-week-old son in April, is competent to stand trial and was sane at the time of the shooting, according to a Bennington psychiatrist.

Dr. James Timmons told listeners Monday at a hearing in District Court that Remington was mentally competent but that her mental state may suffer as the trial date moves closer.

A trial 'may pose a serious threat to her mental well-being,' Timmons said. If her mental state changes her trial may be postponed or canceled. Judge Robert Myers ordered a new evaluation by Timmons and Remington's doctor Ronnie L. Burak, to be completed by July 22.

No trial date had been set but State's Attorney Richard Kelley would like to go to trial by mid-August. The defense said Monday that was too soon.

Timmons also found that Remington was 'not overtly insane at the time of the crime,' according to Kelley."

There was silence on the other end of the line.

I understood how Jeff felt. The community reaction toward Michele was outrage. There were a few gun-toting citizens who would have formed a posse if they thought they could get away with it. This was the most "exciting" story to hit Bennington, and I felt that Calvin Pirk, the *Banner* reporter had not actually misquoted, but had shaded the article in a way that would fan the flames. Nowhere in the article was there a mention that Jim Timmons did not believe Michele "had the mental state required for the offense charged." This was what concerned me when I first read the Timmons report. It would have been much clearer if he had simply said, "Under the meaning of the Vermont statute, at the time of the shooting Mrs. Remington was legally insane," but he didn't.

"Has Michele read this?" I asked.

"Unfortunately yes. She just insists on reading the *Banner* every day. I tried to distract her but it didn't work."

I knew Michele had been present at the hearing, but I suspected that what she heard and what came out in print "sounded" a little different to her.

"How is she?"

"I don't know. I mean, I know she's upset but she's quiet. She didn't cry, but I think she's scared. I mean I know she is." Jeff paused and then said, "Would you call her later?"

I had already been thinking that I would.

When I got home at seven there was still plenty of sunshine. I dropped my briefcase in the front hall and walked into the kitchen. A copy of the *Banner* was lying on the table. Under the REMINGTON WAS SANE headline was a rather austere picture of Dr. Timmons. A somewhat larger picture of a smiling Fred Astaire dancing through the air flanked the article on the right.

Ronnie was outside on the deck barbecuing chicken. I didn't say hello; I didn't sit down; I just stood there in the kitchen reading.

"Is that you?" She must have heard a noise through the kitchen door.

"Yes, honey." I continued reading. A few seconds later she walked through the door.

"Not a very optimistic article as far as Michele's concerned," she said. "And why did they say I was Michele's doctor?"

"It was a mistake—but then it does seem to fit with the rest of the article doesn't it? There's a lot that they didn't get right."

Ronnie then asked, "How's Michele?"

"I can't imagine she's anything but miserable right now."

"Go ahead, I have some baked potatoes that will take another twenty minutes."

Michele answered the phone. "Jeff told me you were going to call. I was real upset—that article really did screw it up."

This was the second time I'd heard anger in her voice. In a way I was glad to hear it. But it was tired sounding, sort of anger with a sigh. She didn't dwell on the article but shifted subjects. "Mom and dad—well, my whole family—have been talking to us about Mr. Henry. It's not that they think he's a bad lawyer, it's just that they felt that I need someone who's really experienced, who can deal with this sort of case."

I felt a sense of relief. "What do you think?" I asked her.

"Well," she said, "at the hearing it almost seemed that the judge was too familiar with Mr. Henry. I don't know—somehow he didn't question things."

"How does Jeff feel?"

"I think he finally agrees, especially after the hearing, but we don't know who to get or how we're going to pay someone. Mr. Henry didn't ask for a lot of money, but I'm sure a stranger will."

In the background I heard Michele's doorbell ring. Her parents had arrived.


Philip and Helen Cort later told me that they had been frantic with worry about Michele's legal situation. Norma had been speaking with a number of friends familiar with the legal community, trying to get the name of a good attorney. She finally identified two lawyers who worked together in Burlington, Vermont. Knowing that Jeff and Michele might be upset by their intrusion, the Corts had gone ahead anyway and called Norman Blais and Mark Keller. They described their daughter's situation. Blais and Keller were interested, but they wanted to speak with Michele directly.

Helen did most of the talking. She told Michele and Jeff about the conversation that she and Philip had had with the attorneys, all the while watching Jeff carefully, concerned that he would be upset. To her surprise he wasn't. Both he and Michele were appreciative. "We've been talking about this," Jeff said, "but we're not sure how we can afford to get a different attorney."

Philip Cort had always been a hardworking man of modest means. He listened quietly as his wife spoke and as his daughter and son-in-law responded. Then, from his coat pocket he withdrew an envelope and handed it to Jeff. In it were fifty crisp one hundred dollar bills.

# 34

On the surface all seemed to be going well. In a few days Jeff and Michele would be going to Burlington to meet Norman Blais and Mark Keller. The newspaper article declaring Michele sane was eight days old.

It was late when I finally left the office and headed home for dinner. Ronnie and Eli had called earlier; they were going to the movies. I looked forward to the quiet, relaxing with some mindless TV and low-fat spaghetti.

I backed out of the office driveway and rolled the windows down. The air was soft and the nine o'clock summer sky was very Maxfield Parrish—a luminescent blue struggling against night's darkness. I felt at peace.

A few minutes later, just as the pasta began to soften, the phone rang. It was a call I expected to get some day, but not then.

Selma at the answering service was apologetic. "I'm sorry to disturb you—I know you just left the office but this sounded urgent. Peggy Glick at the Jasper Company called and asked us to get you right away. She said it was about Michele."

Peggy Glick was Michele's supervisor. A few weeks earlier, just two months after the tragedy, Michele had gone back to work. The weeks of inactivity and confinement in her small apartment had been oppressive. She had to get out. When she had stopped working a few months earlier she had been on the three to eleven shift. It was to that time slot that she returned.

The Jasper Company makes electrical parts, especially capacitors for various kinds of appliances. Part of the process involves the careful wrapping of a core of alternating layers of electrically conductive and nonconductive materials. The exact number of layers is important, and it is difficult to get the wrapping to proceed smoothly and within tolerance. Michele was quite skillful.

During her first few weeks back, the work itself was going well, but the attitude of other employees ranged from apprehensive to aloof to venomous. In was a mean-spirited environment and no one but Peggy Glick would really talk or interact. At meal break Michele sat alone; women would pass without a word and move quickly to a different table.

Bennington College anthropology professor Kenneth Kensinger had lived with the Cashinahua Indians of Eastern Peru for a number of years. He once described for me an experience he had that stuck in my mind. Inadvertently violating an important tribal rule, his punishment had been ostracism, a punishment exceeded in severity only by death or exile in Cashinahua law. For three months Kensinger was a nonperson. No one spoke to him or responded to him in any way. For all intents and purposes he was invisible, absolutely isolated. "You can't imagine the pain of this experience," he said. "Nothing in my life before or since has come close."

Every day I expected Michele to call me and say that she couldn't continue to work. Every day the call did not come. I wasn't sure why. Probably, I thought, a combination of courage, stubbornness, and most of all numbness.

This layer of emotional insulation was doing a good job of

protecting her—most of the time. Occasionally, however, the dike would spring a leak and she would show her pain. Then, like a self-sealing tire that had taken a nail, she would vulcanize and keep on rolling.

I doubted that could continue. One day no thumb would be large enough and no self-sealant strong enough to stop reality. "Maybe this is the day," I thought to myself.

After a few rings someone picked up. "Jasper Company."

"May I speak to Peggy Glick please?"

"Is this Dr. Burak?"

"Hold on—I'll get her." About twenty seconds elapsed and then a very concerned voice on the other end of the line was explaining the urgency of the call. "Something is very wrong with Michele. She just can't seem to pull herself together. A little while ago she began to cry, she won't say what's wrong—she's just been sobbing. I have to tell you I've really been amazed. Up till now she's been doing okay, but she is a mess and she wants to go home. I called there and got no answer—she shouldn't be alone. So I asked her if I could call you and she said okay. Will you speak with her?"

"Sure," I said, "and thanks. Put her on." There was a bit of delay and then Michele was on the line. Before I said anything she said, "I'll be okay, I really didn't want to bother you."

"You're not. Just tell me what's going on."

"I don't know. I was all right when I came in. Nothing really happened, then I just started to cry."

She sounded with every word that the tears would burst through again.

"How do you feel right now?"

"Oh . . ." her voice tailed off. I had the feeling that she wanted to say she was okay but it was too much. After a few seconds she began to try again and through the tears sobbed out, "I'm sorry."

Peggy was probably standing nearby and Michele is a very private person. I had the feeling that she didn't want to talk on the phone.

"Sounds like you're too upset to continue working."

"I guess so."

"Something very important is upsetting you. I want to help and we need to talk—and it shouldn't wait."

"I don't want to bother you. I'll just go home." She tried to sound calm but it didn't work. The hairs on the back of my neck were standing at attention. For the first time since I had met Michele I was worried that she might try to take her life again. There was no way I could let her go home. Maybe she would even need to be back in the hospital, but I would cross that bridge later. First we had to talk face to face.

"I can hear how upset you are. It's important that we talk now—and stop with this bothering me. I told you you're not. How you're doing is important to me, and I just know that this is a time when we need to get together. You can't talk me out of it. If you feel you can't come over to the office, I'll meet you there."

There was a brief pause, then to my relief she said, "I can come to your office."

"Great. I'll meet you in fifteen minutes."

"Okay."


As Michele was settling down on the small sofa in my office I could tell she was still near tears. Her eyes were red and I knew she had been crying all the way over. I should have asked Peggy to bring her, but I hadn't. That she made it without incident was luck, but she was here in one piece.

It took a while. She apologized, she fidgeted, she took off her shoes and sat in the lotus position, she spoke about the environment at work, she cried some more. Then it came out. "I just couldn't do it—I tried but I couldn't do it. The man seemed so matter of fact that I couldn't even tell him I wasn't coming. But I knew I wouldn't get there."

"Where?" I asked.

"To view Joshua's headstone."

Silence. So I repeated her words, "Josh's headstone?"

She shook her head yes. I waited. She began to sob. Tears rolled down her cheeks and onto her lap. The box of Kleenex sat half full on the small table next to the sofa. She could have leaned over and reached it, but I got up, walked over and handed it to her. She clutched a few tissues and kept the box next to her. Her glasses came off as she dabbed at her eyes and continued to sob.

I just waited. It felt like half an hour but it was probably only two minutes. When she looked up again the tears had stopped momentarily. "Two weeks ago Jeff and I ordered Joshua's headstone. Somehow it seemed disconnected from Joshua. Somehow I thought it was going to take a few months and I wouldn't have to think about it. But it's ready and I can't believe it. I just couldn't even think of seeing it. It's too real . . ." As her words trailed off she began to cry again, silently this time.

She tried a few times to resume talking, but the tears would flow and she would stop. Little by little, bits and pieces came out. "I just can't do it . . . The man sounded so matter of fact, as if I should come up to check the color of the paint for the dining room before he continued . . . This is too real—too real . . . I don't think I'll ever be able to visit the cemetery . . . Jeff thinks I should see it to 'get it over with,' but I'll never get it over with . . . How could this have happened?"

Michele's pain filled the room. It almost seemed hard to breathe. Words from me felt trite and unnecessary. But being there with her was important.

"I took his life," she said in a whisper, "how can I look at that stone?" No answer was required. Michele was silent.

As the evening went by Michele became less agitated. Both

of us were tired. I hadn't pushed her to talk about Josh or memories any more than she wished. I didn't know if she actually recovered parts of the missing hours of that tragic Saturday, but if she did she gave no indication.

People communicate in ways I don't pretend to understand. I was there because I cared. I did not see Michele as a villain and understood that she was a victim. I could not always fight Michele's demons, or be her strength, but that night if she had been alone she might have been swallowed whole by the whale of guilt and self-hate.

Michele and I had been together for a few hours. She seemed calmer and the crying had stopped. Still, I was very concerned. Three months earlier, when Josh was alive, her life had been difficult but not impossible or hopeless by any objective yardstick, yet all she could think of was suicide. She nearly succeeded. Now, on this beautiful summer's eve with thoughts of Joshua's headstone emphasizing that she had taken her son's life, it seemed almost understandable that she might think of suicide again. My gut was telling me this was not the case. But I needed to be sure. "Michele, this has been a harrowing day. I'm glad you let Peggy call me. Please, always call me anytime you have to. I mean it!" She knew. She nodded. A good sign. I continued.

"I'm still worried about tonight, the long hours ahead, and then tomorrow and the next day. What do you think you are going to do?"

"Jeff is probably at home now, I'll be all right."

"And tomorrow?" I asked again.

"Well, I think I'll go back to work—I couldn't stand the thought of being in the apartment."

"What about the headstone?"

"I just can't look at it right now. Jeff can take care of it."

The hairs on the back of my neck, which had been at attention when we began to meet and had been somewhat oblique during the past hour, now settled into their proper place. "It sounds as though you're feeling a little better and I'm glad, but I need to know if you have any thoughts about taking your own life again?''

She wasn't surprised by the question. ''I thought you were leading up to that. No—I'm not going to do that, I tried twice and it didn't work. Somehow I feel like it's just not meant to happen.'' I thought she was telling the truth.

I picked up the phone and dialed Michele's number. As the ringing began I handed it to her. Jeff was home.


It was about midnight when I finally ate my pasta. I was ravenous.

# 35 🍂

Burlington, Vermont, is a lovely city of 40,000 situated on the shores of Lake Champlain not too far from the Canadian border. New construction dances with turn-of-the-century architecture, and the major presence of the University of Vermont contributes to an air of youth and vitality. The law firm of Blais, Cain, Keller & Fowler is located in one of those turn-of-the-century buildings on College Street.

As soon as Norman Blais and Mark Keller replaced John Henry the pace began to quicken. Early on the morning of July 23, the two men transferred an infant seat, tennis rackets, balls, and children's toys to the trunk of Keller's VW Rabbit, stopped for coffee to go at a Dunkin Donuts on the outskirts of Burlington, and drove two and a half hours south through Middlebury, Brandon, Rutland, and Manchester, arriving at my office in Bennington at nine-thirty.

In light of the legal profession's aggressive stance on malpractice many physicians distrust and dislike lawyers generically. As a law school graduate I don't harbor some of that automatic antagonism. What I was worried about was whether or not these two men would be able to provide Michele with a solid defense effort. The stakes were very high.

*   *   *

From the moment Norm Blais and Mark Keller walked into my office the feeling was good. (It always intrigues me how this happens.) Both men were pleasant, but all business. After brief introductions they got right to the point. "We need to know if you think that Michele really understood what she was doing at the time of the shooting?"

"No," I said.

"Are you familiar with the Vermont statute regarding insanity?"

"Somewhat."

"Would you like to refresh your memory?"

"Sure."

Mark Keller pulled a copy of the statute from his briefcase and handed it to me. I read it quickly. He waited until I finished and said, "Under the law do you think Michele was not guilty?"

In my heart I had no doubt. I answered "Yes." They glanced at each other—relieved. If Michele's own therapist hadn't been able to say "not guilty" their case would have been extremely difficult.

That first conversation lasted about forty-five minutes. Both men seemed to know their way around the insanity defense. Blais and Keller had worked together as state's attorneys in the late seventies and early eighties. Both were thirty-seven years old. Beyond that they were not at all alike. Blais is round; Keller is lean. Blais is balding and mustachioed; Keller has a John Kennedy mop of neatly groomed brown hair and is clean-shaven. Blais is soft-spoken with a quiet demeanor; Keller is fast with words, determined and aggressive. They made a good team.

Mark Keller called a few days later to ask if I had ever heard of Dr. Roberta Apfels, a psychiatrist who was an expert in postpartum disorders. I hadn't. "Michele's sister Joan came up with her name," Mark said. "Dr. Apfels is a clinical professor at Harvard and has impeccable credentials. Norm and I feel that a third opinion would be helpful." He continued, "Your views are clear. Dr. Timmons will testify in our favor, but he just doesn't seem as firm."

Within the week Michele, Jeff, and the Corts were traveling east on Route 2 across Massachusetts headed for Metropolitan Hospital in Waltham, and an appointment with Dr. Apfels. The fact that she had responded so quickly led me to believe that she was very interested.

Dr. Apfels's report of that meeting also came quickly. She had carefully laid out the history of the tragedy, detail by detail, point by point. Little had escaped her attention. Although I was aware of everything she had said, seeing it summarized this way was striking. At every road's divide along the path to this tragedy the wrong circumstance prevailed, the wrong choice was made, the wrong direction was taken. One minor alteration in this uncanny chain of events might have stopped the dominoes. God had never smiled.

When I reached the heart of Dr. Apfels's report her words were welcome:

> I have detailed the history above because I think therein lie many examples to substantiate my conclusion that Mrs. Remington has had a major psychotic depression. The months postpartum are considered the most vulnerable time in a woman's life for major mental illness. Women who have not been psychotic before are something like eight times more likely to develop psychosis postpartum, and those with the family history or personal history of mental illness have an even greater likelihood. Hormonal changes following delivery, social and psychological factors all contribute to increase the chance of psychotic decompensation.
>
> Even regarding this statistical probability, Mrs. Remington has been suffering from a major depression from her third trimester of

pregnancy. She and her husband confirm that she has "not been herself" and has been incapable of having fun since that time. Consider the diagnostic criteria for major episode:

A. Dysphoric mood, loss of interest and pleasure in all or almost all unusual activities and pastimes.

B. At least four of the following symptoms every day for a period of at least two weeks: Poor appetite, insomnia, psychomotor retardation or agitation, loss of interest or pleasure or decreased sex drive, loss of energy or fatigue, feelings of worthlessness, self-reproach or excessive guilt, complaints or evidence of diminished ability to think not associated with loosened associations or incoherence, recurrent thoughts of death, suicide, wishes to be dead or suicide attempt.

C. Mood-incongruent delusion or hallucination and bizarre behavior do not dominate the picture.

D. Not superimposed on Schizophrenia, Schizophreniform Disorder or Paranoid Disorder.

E. Not due to Organic Mental Disorder or Uncomplicated Bereavement.

Michele has all of the features of a major depression. She has also during these past eight months demonstrated a tendency seen for the past few years in her "premenstrual syndrome" to depersonalize or dissociate. Depersonalization involves an alteration in the perception or experience of the self so that the usual sense of one's reality is temporarily lost or changed. The individual experiences feeling mechanical or as if in a dream. There is a feeling of not being in complete control of one's actions or senses while, to the outside observer, the individual maintains grossly intact reality testing. Amnesia is also a part of Dissociative Disorders; it is the failure to recall the entirety of events for a circumscribed period of time, usually surrounding a profoundly disturbing event.

The tendency to depersonalize can be part of depression, and I believe depression to be largely the basis of Mrs. Remington's dissociative experiences. This alteration in perception occurs as a defense mechanism by which the individual deals with the intense psychic or physical pain. We see it most markedly in Michele Remington around the unplanned shooting of her son. Also, she probably dissociated when she saw the bloody show heralding danger in labor; she ultimately acted appropriately in going to the hospital, but was not able to use the information she knew to act immediately. The twenty-six hours of labor and the "not soaking in" of the dangers to the infant at the delivery time are further examples of depersonalization. This is a state that is psychogenic, but not consciously or deliberately induced. It is made worse by (1) fatigue (Michele had been sleep-deprived for eight months), (2) chemical imbalance (hormone changes in pregnancy and after, and whatever drugs were given during labor and delivery) and (3) other organic factors—e.g., fever, infection. While there is no hard evidence of an organic process we do know that Michele felt ill in the days preceding the shooting with a possible viral syndrome and that she took sleeping medication that may not have been fully cleared from her system—all adding to the psychotic depression, distortion of reality, depersonalization and ultimate tragic outcome.

. . . While Michele Remington is superficially able to stand trial, i.e., she has good reality testing and is competent to understand the Court's situation, I believe that the trial at this time could compound this already tragic story.

# 36

The state's attorney's office is part of a modern office and court complex on Memorial Drive. A quarter mile past the complex is the start of a twenty-mile stretch of new highway, a twin ribbon of road that dramatically slices through the mountains linking Bennington with its northern neighbor, Manchester. On winter Fridays the road is busy with skiers. In the nonskiing months, streams of cars head north from Connecticut and New York bringing shoppers by the thousands who wish to spend money aggressively in the various Manchester outlets. Mark had just driven those twenty miles south in a little more than fifteen minutes. He was on time, but Kelley was late. We had a few minutes to talk.

"How are you feeling about the deposition?" Mark asked.

"Actually I'm a little nervous. I know Kelley can be aggressive, and this case is so visible around here that I suspect he's feeling a lot of pressure."

"Well, you're right—but he's in a very tough position right now," Mark paused as if he was considering what to say next. "Kelley is in a tough position because he has a murder with the smoking gun, yet the evidence of insanity is piling up. Although it wasn't strongly worded, Timmons did support our position. I also think Kelley expected Bill Woodruff at the University of Vermont to support his position. He was listed by Kelley as a prosecution witness yet we've seen no report. Why? Well, I bumped into Dr. Woodruff a few weeks ago and we talked. He had been involved in a similar case about ten years ago and felt strongly that the insanity defense was appropriate. He knew the facts of Michele's case, probably from reports that Kelley sent, and I'm almost sure that he has called Kelley and told him that Michele was probably insane, that he would be happy to see her, but doubted he would find differently from Timmons and Apfels." Keller continued, "A few days ago I called Kelley on the phone and we had a long talk. I know and he knows that you can never predict a jury's decision—but our position is becoming stronger. I think your deposition is going to tip the scales in our favor even more. And he's got to be frustrated. Since I was a prosecutor for many years myself, I know how he feels." Keller was on a roll, talking rapidly. "I said, 'Dick, this is not a matter of strategy, it's a matter of doing the right thing. I think Norm and I have a strong case for insanity because Michele truly didn't know what she was doing, because she had been depressed and psychotic. Timmons said so, Apfels said so, Burak is going to say the same thing, and I think that every psychiatrist you ask would say the same thing. The fact is she's not a criminal.' At that point he said to me, 'Mark, I know what you're saying, but this community is outraged and they expect action. At the very least I am going to have to pursue this as much as I can before I can consider backing down.'"

Mark looked at me. "Kelley's not really a bad guy—he's stuck." Then he smiled, with a twinkle in his eye. "So I tried to help him, I told him a story." Keller continued: "In 1978, on one of the first beautiful days of spring, everybody in Burlington was outside enjoying the weather during lunch. A young woman was sitting with some friends on a grassy lawn at the top of Church Street. John Heinz, a stranger, a drifter, who happened to be a black man in this very white town, walked up to this young woman who he didn't know and with absolutely no warning struck her in the head with a pipe and killed her. There was no motive—nothing. Maybe this sort of thing happens in other places, but not in Burlington. The community wanted a lynching, and I was the state's attorney at the time. Just like Kelley in Michele's case. Anyway, Heinz was crazy, totally insane. Everybody who had contact with him knew it—the police, the physicians—and as a matter of fact it was Dr. Woodruff who was the psychiatrist that evaluated him. There was no question. But I was upset—I felt like I couldn't let this man get away with this horrible crime, I felt that a jury might convict even with the evidence of his insanity." Mark paused for a few seconds and I asked, "So what happened, did you get a conviction?"

"We didn't go to trial. Heinz went into the state hospital for psychiatric care. It almost killed me to do that, but that's what happened. And you know why I made the decision to accept the insanity plea?" He didn't wait for me to answer, "Because it was the right thing to do. Because our laws require that somebody has to have the capacity in a rational, nondistorted, noncrazy way to understand what they are doing, to intend to do it, and to have control of themselves before we can convict them as criminals. Even so, I might still have gone for the conviction if it hadn't been for Norm Blais. At the time he was the deputy state's attorney. I was out for blood. He came into my office one morning, closed the door and let me have it. I've never seen him as upset before or since. He said 'Mark, you've got to do the right thing. You know damn well that Heinz is crazy. He should be put away—but according to law. Don't act on your anger. Don't go for a big notch in your gun. Don't compromise your principles. You know what's right. Do the right thing!'"

Mark looked away briefly and then right at me again. "I knew he was right. And I did what was right and I've never regretted it."

As he had been talking Mark became impassioned, then suddenly, as if he remembered why he was telling the story, his tone changed. "So I said to Kelley the same thing that Norm said to me, 'You know what's right. Michele did not know what was going on—she's not a criminal and you know that!' Actually it was even tougher for me because Heinz wasn't a victim himself, and Michele is. Heinz was just a crazy son of a bitch and it galled me not to go to trial, but it was the right thing." Mark stopped.

After a moment I asked, "So what did Kelley say?"

"Well, he said he understood, but he felt he couldn't let go unless he was absolutely sure that everyone would understand there was no recourse, no disagreement at all about Michele's sanity. So I told him I too had the same feelings about Heinz and I told him what I'd done to get clear. I called the National District Attorney's Association and asked for the name of a forensic psychiatrist who they knew was very conservative, very tough, maybe less likely to find someone insane." Mark smiled again. "We know who the tough guys are—they referred me to the Manhattan district attorney's office and someone there suggested that I speak to Dr. Stanley Brodsky, a psychiatrist with a great deal of forensic experience who was very conservative and highly respected. I didn't know if it was a joke but the guy told me that Brodsky found 'Son of Sam' sane. So I figured if he told me Heinz was insane I would accept the plea of insanity. We flew Brodsky up to Burlington. He examined Heinz, found him insane, and that was it. So I suggested to Kelley that he might get in touch with Brodsky."

"Will he do it?"

"Well, he didn't say too much, but I have a hunch he will. I've been told by a few people in Burlington that he has already made some calls asking about the Heinz case, so I know he was listening. And I think your deposition will add fuel to the fire."

It was about eleven-fifteen. My deposition had been scheduled for eleven, but I had been so absorbed by Mark's story that I hadn't noticed the time. The door of the state's attorney's office opened at that moment, and a tall, well-dressed, attractive woman with long dark hair began to walk toward us. I didn't know who she was, but I hadn't been looking forward to my time with Kelley and I remember wishing she would depose me instead. My wish came true. "Good morning," she said. "You must be Dr. Burak?" I nodded.

"And you're Mr. Keller?"

"Yes," Mark answered.

"I'm Lainie Hutton, the deputy state's attorney. Dick was unfortunately held up in court, and we didn't want to inconvenience you so I'm going to do the deposition."

I probably smiled.

# 37

As the earth tilted the comfortable warm days of summer turned cool; the famous Vermont color was glorious and then the trees of autumn were barren.

It had been gray on the day of my deposition, and now, three days later, there was still no sign of the sun. Michele had a regularly scheduled appointment, and from the moment she came into my office I knew something was up. She usually began with a little small talk, slid into medium talk, until eventually she would open up. Today there was no warm up; she came right to the point and seemed agitated.

"Kelley offered me a deal."

I had been hoping. I asked, "What do you mean?"

"He's willing to reduce the murder charge to manslaughter and recommend probation with no jail time. Mark just told me about it yesterday." She looked at me, questioning but silent. I asked first, "What do you think?"

Michele lowered her head, then raised it again as she spoke. "I think Jeff almost wants me to take the deal—no trial—no jail—and we already owe so much in legal fees—Norm and Mark are worth every penny, but I know Jeff's worried about the additional cost of going through a trial. And then, of course, who knows what will happen if we do get into a trial? Mark and Norm think our case is strong, but they've made it clear that you never know what a jury will decide until it is really over. I think Mark really doesn't want me to take the deal. Norm is trying very hard to be absolutely neutral. I think that Jeff would really like me to take it, but he's trying not to push."

I knew I would be asked for my vote, but I was going to try very hard not to give it. Michele needed this time to explore her own feelings without influence. This really had to be her decision.

I too believed that she had a strong case, but I understood that if she faced the music she had every right to be afraid. The law, which often seems so specific, so rigid, so technical and rulebound, is really putty in the hands of those who are legal enforcers and decision makers. From the trooper who enforces the fifty-five mile per hour speed limit, to the juror or judge who decides whether a woman who shot and killed her infant will go to jail—the facts and rules of law are just pieces of information that go through the grinder of mood, perspective, and religious belief. The decision based upon the very same facts can be different from one person to the next and sometimes even with the same person, different from one day to the next.

"Sorry officer, I guess I was doing sixty-five, I was thinking about a problem at home and I guess I wanted to get there quick. I'm sorry."

"That's ten miles over, sir, I'm going to give you this ticket for excessive speed. Instructions as to what to do are on the back. Any questions? Have a nice day."

"Sorry officer, I guess I was going sixty-five, I was thinking about a problem at home and I guess I wanted to get there quick. I'm sorry."

"That's ten miles over, sir, but I appreciate your honesty and your attitude. I'm going to give you a warning, but the next time you might not be so lucky. So drive a little slower—huh? Have a nice day."

Judges and juries are no worse, no better, no more precisely predictable than the lone trooper. It is never over in a courtroom until the fat lady sings and all too often it's not your tune.

In October of 1986, Sharon Comitz, a young Pennsylvania woman, was tried for the drowning death of her infant son, Garrett. Sharon elected to have a court trial without a jury. Like Michele, her defense attorney sought to prove that she was suffering from a serious biologically based psychiatric illness directly related to the birth of her son. In Sharon's case, this was the same sort of illness that she had suffered five years earlier following the birth of her daughter. At that time she had become suicidal.

Even the psychologist who served as witness for the prosecution in Sharon's case acknowledged her illness: "In our society mothers do not kill their children unless they are seriously disturbed." Although the evidence for postpartum depression was strong, it didn't convince Judge Braun:

> "She was responsible for killing another human being and it seems to me that a period of incarceration is appropriate for someone with postpartum depression as well as it is for someone without postpartum depression."

He sentenced Sharon Comitz to a prison term of eight to twenty years.

I looked across at Michele, finding it hard to believe that the same would happen to her. I didn't know the Comitz case intimately, didn't have a transcript of the testimony, and wondered if the information was presented as clearly as it should have been. In addition, there were two other striking differences between her and Michele: The first was that Michele had almost succeeded in taking her own life while Comitz had on this occasion not attempted suicide; second, Comitz had initially told the police a confusing story as though she were trying to cover up what she had done. Still, there was little doubt that she, like Michele, suffered significantly from an altered mental state.

After Garrett died, Glen Comitz was in a state of shock. His anger eventually subsided and he grieved for his wife. She was as much a victim as he, and he understood that the woman who took Garrett's life was not the Sharon that he knew. The insanity defense was society's attempt to be humane with individuals who acted criminally but were not of a criminal mind and were not in control. Glen believed that this was his wife's situation, and Judge Braun's decision was a second nightmare. Shattered by the loss of his son, he was now deprived of his wife as well. As was the case with Michele and Jeff, he and Sharon needed each other more than ever. He had to appeal the decision.

Glen Comitz turned first to Daniel Katkin, head of the Department of Administration of Justice at nearby Penn State University. Fortyish, soft-spoken, prematurely gray, and very insightful, Katkin listened quietly as Comitz spun his tale of woe. He was very interested.

During the next few months Katkin identified seventeen other cases of infanticide that occurred during the preceding five years. In every one of these eighteen cases (including Sharon's), claims of an altered postpartum mental state were well supported. The score card, however, read nine convictions and nine acquittals (although the acquittals were usually followed by psychiatric hospitalizations).

"Michele" I said, "you just told me what Jeff thinks. What do you think?"

There was no pause. She looked me in the eye and for me that moment will forever define what is meant by a "moment of truth." "I just can't do it," she said, "I can't take the deal." She paused, "I know that may be stupid—I could lose and I don't think I could live with myself if I did, or for that matter I don't think I could survive in jail—and I know it will mean we owe a lot more money—but I can't do it. All my life I would have to live with the conviction. Even if it were manslaughter I would have to live with it. It's silly, I know, but I think I can make it if I don't have that hanging over my head. I just can't take the deal, I'm going to have to take my chances.

# 38 ~

Dr. Stanley Brodsky listened carefully to Richard Kelley explain the circumstances of Michele's case. "Mr. Kelley," he said, "Before I make a trip to Vermont, why don't you let me review the written reports that you have so far." Kelley agreed. The reports were sent by Federal Express that day. Three days later Richard Kelley received a call. "The evidence supporting insanity in this case is extremely strong. I doubt very much that my evaluation would differ."

Kelley took a deep breath and made a quick decision. He would not ask Brodsky to travel to Vermont. Instead, he asked for a letter reflecting his opinion based upon his review of the records.

January 12, 1987

Re: *State v. Remington*

Richard A. Kelley, Esq.
State's Attorney
State of Vermont
Bennington County State's Attorney
One Veterans Memorial Drive
Bennington, Vermont 05201

Dear Mr. Kelley:

In accordance with your request, I have reviewed copies of reports, transcripts and documents involved in this case . . .

Based on a review of the above material, it is my opinion with reasonable psychiatric certainty that the Defendant, Michele Remington, was suffering from Major Depression at the time of the alleged crime and that the defense of insanity can be supported. Because of the severity of her depression and her suicidal intent, she was unable to conform her behavior to the requirements of the law or to appreciate the wrongfulness of her actions.

It is evident that Michele Remington suffered from a serious depression following childbirth, which was apparent both to physicians as well as to family members. Her symptoms did meet the requirements for Major Depression in accordance with the criteria stated in the DSM III.

It is apparent that at the time of the alleged crime, Michele Remington was in the throes of a very serious depression, was suicidal and committed a homicidal act in conjunction with a very serious suicidal attempt with the clear intent to take her life.

It is not uncommon in a woman who is suffering from a Major Depression in the weeks following childbirth that a homicidal attack on the baby can be seen as an extension of an overriding suicidal act. In cases like this, the mother is not perceiving a separation between herself and the baby. It is likely in this case that the baby's potential neurological disorder played a significant role in the mother's depression and guilt feelings.

> Signed very truly yours,
> STANLEY H. BRODSKY, M.D., F.A.P.A.
> Director, Psychiatric Forensic Service of New York

Kelley now knew that he would have no effective rebuttal to the insanity defense. If he were going to continue the prosecution, he would have to depend on the unpredictability of the jury, which in this case could ride a wave of anger to conviction. Richard Kelley agonized.

Mark Keller called me the day after Christmas. "I've spoken to Dick Kelley and we've worked out a solution. We'll provide the court with Dr. Apfels's report, and he'll provide the court with Dr. Brodsky's letter. He would also like to have you testify at the hearing about Michele's mental state at the time of the shooting. Then he would stipulate to the court that the state did not contest the finding of insanity. This would allow Judge Robert Meyers to officially rule that Michele was insane at the time of the shooting, and therefore not guilty according to law. The judge would then want you to provide your opinion about Michele's need for further treatment. What do you think?"

"I can't imagine a better outcome for Michele."

"Neither can I," he said.

The hearing before Judge Meyers was held on January 19. Had this been the trial that the community expected, the courtroom would have been packed. As it was, the number of attendees was small, consisting mostly of members of both Michele's and Jeff's families. This was the first time I had a chance to meet Michele's sister Joan, who had identified Roberta Apfels as a potential expert witness.

My testimony was brief. Kelley asked a few clarifying questions, all in the spirit of cooperation. Then Judge Meyers asked if Michele required hospitalization.

"Not at this time, your honor. Mrs. Remington has been in outpatient therapy on a regular basis and that should continue."

One week later Judge Meyers's written "Decision and Order" was handed down:

"The Defendant herein, a 29-year-old married woman, was charged with murder in the first degree in that on April 4, 1987, she did deliberately, willfully, and with premeditation kill another human being, to wit: Did load a .22 caliber revolver with six rounds of ammunition, placed the barrel on the gun on the chest of another, and pulled the trigger, thereby causing death, in violation of 13 V.S.A. Sect. 2301.

On January 19, 1988, this Court held a hearing to determine whether the Defendant was insane at the time of the alleged offense and, if so, whether she should be hospitalized. Such a hearing was held pursuant to 13 V.S.A. Sect. 4820 . . .

The Court finds and concludes as follows:

1. On April 4, 1987, Jeff Remington, the husband of Defendant herein, was working in the barn of his home on Jefferson Avenue in Bennington, Vermont, when the power went off. He went inside the home with his wife and six-week-old son. He found his wife in a chair holding her side and also holding her son. He observed that his son was not breathing so he ran next door to his brother's apartment for assistance. The infant was taken to the Southwestern Vermont Medical Center.

2. When the child was examined in the Emergency Room it was determined that he was dead. The cause of death was a gun-shot to the chest which exited out the lower back near the spine. The Medical Examiner was of the opinion that the cause of death was a homicide.

3. Officers responding to the Remington home found the Defendant sitting in a chair with her hands against her chest saying, "It wasn't supposed to happen this way." And, "I'm supposed to be dead."

4. A .22 caliber revolver was located on the floor a short distance from the chair in which the Defendant was seated. An examination of the weapon showed that the revolver was fully loaded and had been fired twice.

5. The Defendant was admitted to the Southwestern Vermont Medical Center on April 4, 1987, via the Emergency Room. She underwent an exploratory laparotomy as well as an exploratory of the diaphragm and left lower chest. The surgeon removed a .22 caliber bullet from the body of the Defendant. She survived the surgery in good condition and her postoperative course was uneventful. She was discharged on April 14, 1987.

6. Subsequent to the incident the Defendant was seen by at least

four different psychiatrists who evaluated her for sanity and competency.

7. James Timmons, M.D., of Bennington, Vermont, examined the Defendant and rendered an opinion that at the time of the incident she suffered from postpartum depression with psychosis (298.80 DSM-3). Dr. Timmons is of the opinion that the Defendant did not have the mental state required to commit the offense charged.

8. Roberta J. Apfels, M.D., of Newton, Massachusetts, personally examined the Defendant on July 29, 1987, and submitted an exhaustive report. In the opinion of Dr. Apfels the Defendant was not responsible for her conduct, because she was suffering from psychotic depression, and because of this mental disease, lacked adequate capacity to understand the criminality of her act and lacked the judgment necessary to conform her conduct to the requirements of law. Dr. Apfels diagnosed the Defendant as suffering from Major Depression.

9. Pursuant to the request of the Bennington County State's Attorney, reports, transcripts and documents in the case, including reports of Dr. Apfels and Dr. Timmons were reviewed by Stanley H. Brodsky, M.D., a forensic psychiatrist practicing in Forest Hills, New York. On a review of the material submitted to him, Dr. Brodsky rendered an opinion with reasonable psychiatric certainty that the Defendant was suffering from a Major Depression at the time of the incident and that the defense of insanity can be supported. He is further of the opinion that, because of the severity of her depression and her suicidal intent, she was unable to conform her behavior to the requirements of law or to appreciate the wrongfulness of her actions.

10. Carl Burak, M.D., a Board Certified Psychiatrist practicing in Bennington, Vermont, diagnosed the Defendant as being psychotically depressed at the time of the incident and that such a depression construed a mental disease or defect. In his opinion as a result of the mental depression, the Defendant was not capable of understanding her actions and had no ability to conform her conduct to the requirements of law.

11. Dr. Apfels stated in her report that the Defendant needs continuing treatment for her depression. She further indicated that the current out-patient treatment appears to be working satisfactorily.

12. Dr. Burak testified that the patient is not in need of hospitalization but is in need of further out-patient treatment. He further testified that while the Defendant is at times dysphoric, that is, exhibits a mild form of depression, she is able to meet the normal demands of daily living and is not now in need of hospitalization. Dr. Burak testified that the Defendant can be helped by continued counseling and out-patient treatment.

13. On April 4, 1987, Michele G. Remington, the Defendant herein, did deliberately, willfully and with premeditation shoot another human being, to wit, her infant son, with a .22 caliber revolver thereby causing his death.

### Conclusions of Law

1. Based upon the reports of the examining psychiatrists and the testimony of Carl Burak, the Defendant's treating psychiatrist, the Court concludes as follows:

   (A.) The Defendant at the time of the homicide on April 4, 1987, was suffering from a mental disease or defect, to wit, Major Depression;

   (B.) As a result of such mental disease she lacked adequate capacity to appreciate the criminality of her conduct and the capacity to conform her conduct to the requirements of law.

2. Further, based upon the reports of the examining psychiatrists and the testimony of Dr. Carl Burak, a Board Certified Psychiatrist, the Court concludes that the Defendant is not in need of hospitalization. The Court concludes, however, that the Defendant is in need of ongoing psychiatric care and treatment on an out-patient basis. Accordingly, an order of nonhospitalization is appropriate under the provision of 18 V.S.A. Sect. 7618 (a).

#### ORDER

1. In view of the conclusion that Michele G. Remington, the Defendant herein, was not criminally responsible for her acts committed on April 4, 1987, because of her lack of mental capacity on that date, the Court enters a finding of not guilty by reason of insanity pursuant to law. The information is dismissed.

2. Pursuant to the provisions of 18 V.S.A. Sect. 7618 (a) the Defendant, Michele G. Remington, is ordered to pursue an out-patient course of therapy conducted by a qualified mental health professional for an initial period of ninety days.

3. Dated at Bennington, County of Bennington and State of Vermont on this 26th day of January, 1988, signed ROBERT MEYERS, DISTRIC JUDGE.

# 39 🪶

The Bennington *Banner* ran a small article about Michele's acquittal. The Associated Press picked up the story. One of the newspapers in which it was published was the Boston *Globe*. Susan O'Connell, a Boston attorney and mother of two had experienced postpartum depression following the birth of her second child. She shuddered when she read the brief article about Michele in the *Globe*. Her depression hadn't been as severe, but she had some understanding. She picked up the phone and dialed Lillian Smith, her friend in New York. Lillian agreed that the story was important. She went immediately to her boss, Phil Donahue. He gave her a green light to produce the show.

It was on the evening of February 2 when Jeff Remington called.

"You mean Michele wants to do this?" I couldn't believe it.

"Yes," he said, "we've had a few other requests from TV and radio and one magazine wanted to interview Michele. To this point she has absolutely refused—but she wants to do this."

"Why?"

"Well, we both feel that it may help others to know about our experience. And another thing is, Michele likes Phil Donahue—if it wasn't him she wouldn't even think of doing it. She feels as though he would understand and be fair, and we talked for a long time with Ms. Smith, who was very nice. She said that Mr. Donahue was very interested in doing the show and understood how difficult it would be."

I listened as Jeff spoke, still in disbelief. Michele is such a private person and was so embittered by some of the early articles in the Bennington *Banner* that this was the most unlikely situation I could imagine.

"Even with Donahue's good intentions, Jeff, this is going to be very tough."

"I know," he said, "but both of us feel the same way, we want to do it. But there is one other thing."

"What's that?" I asked.

"Michele told Ms. Smith that she would only go on the show if I was there, if you were there, and also if Mark and Norm were there as well."

I was silent for a few moments and Jeff said, "Are you there?"

"Yes, I am. Is Michele there?"

"Yeah, let me put her on."

There was a noise of the telephone switching hands, then Michele's voice, "Quite a surprise—huh?"

"That's an understatement," I said.

"Well, I thought that you might think that this was a bad idea but somehow I feel like I've got to do it. Ms. Smith seemed truly concerned, and she reassured me that everyone, especially Mr. Donahue, would try to be sensitive to me and were interested in educating the public. I believe her."

The idea of getting the word out about postpartum depression was appealing, but the personal fallout for Michele might be a mess. I had to admit that I felt a little intimidated by the prospect of sitting on the *Donahue* stage. I could flatly refuse to cooperate, and maybe she wouldn't do it—but I might really be depriving her of an opportunity to do some sort of penance in her own way.

"Do you want to think about this for a day or two?" I asked.

"Well, actually, Ms. Smith called yesterday and I have been thinking about it—we've been thinking about it—and we're sure."

"Okay," I said quietly, "what's the next step?"

# 40 ![feather]

The only noise in the room was the soft sound of television cameras moving as Angela Thompson became the focus of attention. It had been five years since she had drowned her second-born child, but she was speaking about the severe postpartum depression she had experienced after the birth of her first child.

"I went through the illness without having any tragic consequences, but during that time I did jump off a bridge. It was after the baby was born, during the postpartum. I could have killed or injured myself severely at that point, and then I got pregnant the second time, which was a planned pregnancy. I went to the obstetrician and explained to him that I had a severe psychotic episode following my first child, and I jumped off a bridge, and I thought my husband was Jesus Christ. His advice to me was not to worry about this happening again. It turned out to be fatal advice in our situation."

Perhaps Angela was misquoting, but for whatever reason I didn't for a second question her story. What I didn't know was whether her doctor had been ignorant about the potential seriousness of a major depressive/psychotic episode, or just overly complacent at having seen too many women who had postpartum depression without a tragic outcome.

Donahue continued his discussion with Angela, wanting to know about the religious preoccupations that had consumed her.

"In my psychotic delusion I believed that Michael represented the devil. I thought that if I drowned the baby then I would kill the devil, but my husband being Jesus Christ would then come and raise up the baby on the third day and the world would know that my husband was Jesus Christ and the world would know that the second coming had come." Angela paused, her eyes glistening with tears. "I really thought my baby would live again." Jeff Thompson stared straight at the floor.

Donahue's voice continued quietly, "So this was not an act of murder, this was an act of redemption."

"Right. This was my calling to the world as the bride of Christ, which is who I believed I was." Angela Thompson reported no history of psychiatric difficulty prior to her first postpartum experience; "No psychosis, no depression, no PMS, no problems with drugs, no problems with any kind of abuse in my family or anything like that."

As I listened to Angela my views of postpartum illness were strengthened. It turned out that she had an underlying vulnerability to mood problems that hadn't blossomed until the stress of her first pregnancy acted as a trigger. During her enforced hospitalizations her doctors recognized that she had bipolar illness (manic-depression), and they began successful treatment with medication, which included lithium. She had been forced to stop the medication during her unexpected third pregnancy in order to protect the fetus. A British physician, Katarina Dalton, had recommended that as a preventive measure she have hormone treatments immediately following delivery. I knew this was not routine operating procedure for my American colleagues, but Angela had done well during her most recent postpartum period. It is possible of course that she would have done well without the hormone treatment. Just because she had two prior episodes of postpartum psychosis did not guarantee that she would have had a repeat episode after her third pregnancy. For reasons no one can explain, sometimes it just doesn't happen.

Had I been in the Thompsons' shoes, however, I damn well would have done what they did.

When Donahue introduced Michele I looked at her and wasn't sure she was going to be able to speak. He drew her out quietly, focusing on her own injury.

"Yes, the bullet was very close to my heart. Dr. Loy told me it missed by millimeters. It passed through my chest and ended up in my back." Michele pointed with her right hand to the area of her left shoulder blade, and "They took it out here."

Donahue shifted his line of questioning to the time of Joshua's delivery.

"Well, I was two weeks overdue. When I got up that morning I knew my water had broken. I felt kind of strange, you know like there was a plastic coating or something and I was in there and nobody could really hear me. It's so hard to explain."

Watching Michele I could see she was struggling. Donahue noticed also. He refocused on Jeff who seemed eager to take over. "After being forced out of work Michele could only lay around the house. We lived on the third floor and Michele couldn't go up and down the stairs and she lay there on the couch—all day, all night. You could see a change coming over her. She began to get really withdrawn. The pregnancy was just going on too long. We have a beagle and she seemed to have a fixation on the dog. She thought the dog always had to go out for a walk and it just got out of hand—completely out of hand."

I glanced at Michele. She was looking at the floor.

Jeff continued "When we went to the hospital the morning her water broke," he quickly turned to Michele, "we had what—twenty-five hours of labor?"

Michele responded quietly, "Close to thirty or more."

"Twenty-five to thirty hours of labor," Jeff picked up again, "Then the doctors finally said 'Okay, it's time. We're going to do something.' They rushed Michele into the delivery room.

They did a forceps delivery, and our son Joshua was born with asphyxia—oxygen deprivation. He was taken two minutes after birth and flown in a helicopter to a hospital about forty-five to fifty miles away and was diagnosed with brain damage and was just one sick little kid." Jeff's voice was on the edge of cracking.

Donahue gave Jeff a moment of relief, asked if he had a chance to see the baby.

"I was not there for the delivery. I saw my son Joshua just as he was in an incubator being loaded onto the helicopter."

As Jeff acknowledged his terror the audience was intensely interested. I was so engrossed in watching their faces, I was surprised when I heard my name.

"Dr. Carl Burak—you are Michele's psychiatrist. You feel, among other things, that women who kill their babies under these circumstances should be treated as very ill people and not criminals."

My mouth opened and words came out. "Absolutely. I believe that we're dealing with an illness that is medical in many respects. Stress may push somebody, but postpartum depression, like all depression, reflects an underlying biochemical vulnerability. In other words, whether the stress is a difficult pregnancy, a difficult marriage, unusually strong hormonal swings following delivery—whatever it is—certain women will be more vulnerable than others."

That was it, all that Donahue apparently wanted from me. He turned to Michele asking about her six weeks with Joshua. She was slow to respond and again Jeff stepped in. "We didn't have six weeks. He was in the hospital for three weeks. Then after Joshua was home Michele was there for two weeks. For the week prior to the shooting she was at her parents' house and I had Joshua. I stayed at our house and Michele was at her mother's. She was so depressed that she simply couldn't function at home. She would just sit and do absolutely nothing. When Joshua cried she would get up and check him, but then she would go back and sit in the chair. She wasn't eating, she wasn't sleeping, she wasn't talking, she wasn't doing anything."

Jeff's words were filled with obvious feeling, a pallet of frustration and sadness. I was watching Michele. She glanced down and I was concerned. She was always distressed when recalling the final days. I could tell that Donahue was aware of this and he didn't push, but he did again invite her to join in.

After a few moments of silence Michele began. "The most significant thing was that I felt cheated. They took him away from me, I didn't even get to hold him. I went to the hospital to have a baby and I came home without one."

With further questioning Michele described her three weeks with Joshua in greater detail. "With me it was like an obsession to make up for that bonding that I lost. I felt cheated. There I was in maternity, other people had their babies and I didn't. So when we brought him home it was like—I tried desperately for that time I lost . . . and the way I was feeling . . . my nerves were jumping outside my skin. Joshua could feel that. I wasn't sleeping. I wasn't eating. When I did eat I forced myself because I was breastfeeding. But I had all I could do to keep the food down most of the time. But I did it for him. It was more desperation than anything." Then Michele looked down as she said, "And I was jealous when Jeff took care of him because Josh seemed to respond so much better."

Donahue understood. Like so many mothers suffering with serious postpartum depression, Michele felt that her baby didn't like her. With some mothers it's just a feeling; with Michele it had been an intense psychotic delusion.

# 41 🪶

Again sensing that Michele had reached her limit, Donahue turned to Jeff, asking him details about the shooting. As he responded, a number of women in the audience began to openly cry.

"I found my wife just hugging her chest like this." He moved his arms in front of him and bent forward. "She wouldn't talk to me, when I shook her all I got was a moan. I looked over and I saw Joshua and he was just white. I knew that was wrong so I grabbed him and kicked down my front door and got my brother and we made a mad dash to the hospital and called the police from there."

Donahue made a critical point, depression is common after the birth of a child, but who could ever imagine that depression, even a serious one, would lead to the sort of tragedy that befell the Remingtons and the Thompsons.

"I saw my wife being depressed," Jeff said, "but you just don't kill your own child. You can't imagine it happening to you and I was living through it. It was so very difficult to live with. We have talked about it often. I still love my wife and I don't blame her, I blame the disease—and maybe some specialists who weren't intelligent enough to spot it. They should have had the information and they didn't have it, or they didn't use it."

Donahue commented on the fact that both couples had remained together through all of this.

Jeff Thompson responded without hesitation. "My wife was sick and she needed help. So we're just helping each other through it."

I was struck by Thompson's words. I glanced to the audience and looked at Glen Comitz, whose wife Sharon was already serving a prison sentence in Pennsylvania for taking the life of their infant son. I had met Glen in the lobby of the hotel earlier in the morning. I looked at these three men—Jeff Remington, Jeff Thompson, and Glen Comitz. All three had been shocked and enraged; all three grieved; all three not only remained with their wives but had become their most understanding and strongest supporters. If these men who had lost their sons did not wish to punish, was that not the strongest signal imaginable that these women who would commit an act of murder in the postpartum were different and needed temperance and understanding? In the end, for Angela and for Michele the system had come through. Each had received help; each had been declared not guilty because in their minds and hearts they had not been criminals. For Sharon Comitz, despite substantial evidence that she too had suffered with significant postpartum depression, the legal system had swept her along the criminal pathway.

While I was reflecting, Donahue had opened the phone lines. A female voice came over the loudspeaker. "My sister is serving a sentence in Vermont for having killed her twins. I'm sure she had postpartum depression. She's served two years and she has seventeen years to go. It's really divided the family—some people in the family don't believe that she could have been crazy, but I know my sister is not a murderer and I just—it just tears me up. She shouldn't be where she is."

As the caller finished Donahue moved briskly across the front of the stage and introduced Lenore Walker, whom I had met just before we went on the air. A clinical psychologist from Denver, Dr. Walker had a great deal of experience with postpartum cases.

Dr. Walker began. "In my opinion a number of women are in jail who shouldn't be there. What happens to you depends not only on what state you did it in—they have different laws—but it's also very much up to an individual judge or prosecutor as to what the outcome is, or even if they're going to prosecute these women. The legal outcome also depends upon the medical or psychological help that women have available to them, and far too many people don't understand that a woman could really be crazy and not look that way. In one case, for example, the woman worked in her family business. They had a restaurant and she was the hostess, and well—people saw her every day. They didn't understand that she was suffering so intensely. You can be mentally ill and still hide it for short periods of time—like showing people to their seats in a restaurant. Now her family knew something was wrong, but much like the stories you heard they didn't know what to do. And it's happened throughout the ages. We should know that some women are going to be in trouble. We could identify them if we paid enough attention."

I wanted to stand up and cheer.

# 42 ～

After Dr. Walker's comments Donahue bounced up the aisle and tipped the microphone toward a middle-aged woman, now standing. "Michele, you stated for three weeks when you had your child you could hardly drag yourself out of bed, you couldn't eat, you were severely depressed and your husband noticed this too. I wonder why you didn't get some kind of help. That's not an average everyday postpartum blues."

Michele answered, "I had people coming and trying to take care of things. My mother walked into the house about two weeks before [the shooting] and almost passed out when she saw me sitting in the chair. She said I was as white as a ghost and I was just sitting there with the shades down in the dark. So she called my doctor—the doctor who delivered the baby, and pleaded with the nurses to give me an appointment that day. She said, 'You have to see her, she looks awful.' But they wouldn't do it—wouldn't fit me in. They minimized it and said she's having the 'baby blues'; she'll get over it."

Michele's words dramatically hung in the air. With impeccable timing, Donahue suddenly switched focus to the insanity defense, noting how all of America had been fed up after Hinckley used this defense with some success after his shooting of President Reagan. Walking over to a prematurely white-haired gentleman (like Donahue himself) who was sitting on the stage, he introduced Daniel Katkin, professor of the Administration of Justice at Penn State University.

"The insanity defense is an absolutely essential element of the legal system," Katkin said. "If someone's behavior is not under their control, and if we can't say what they did was a product of an evil state of mind, then it is not appropriate for us to treat them punitively. Let's say you're driving down the street, you stop at a red light, somebody opens the door—sits down next to you—puts a gun to your head and says 'I'm going to rob a bank, you drive me there.' In a sense a woman with a serious post-partum psychosis is like the driver of that car. Some monster takes over and they're really not responsible."

Donahue took another viewer call, from a woman who sounded very young. I felt the hairs on the back of my neck rise as she began to speak. "I have a baby right now and she's five months old and I'm not sure what to do. I'm seventeen years old and I'm living with my parents while waiting to get married. Sometimes I feel like things would be better if the baby wasn't around. I love her dearly and I'm just—I'm just so torn up inside, I don't know what to do."

A year earlier it had been Michele who was floating on the River Styx. She was perhaps not in exactly the same boat as this young caller, but she had been traveling in the same current. What if Michele had turned on this *Donahue* back then? What if she had seen other women who suffered and lost the battle? What if Jeff had been watching? What if her parents had been watching? What if Dr. Murray's nurses had been watching?

On the air Donahue pleaded with this young woman not to hang up. And it was one of those sweet magical days when luck is on your side. Lenore Walker practices psychology in Denver. The caller lived in nearby Albuquerque, and Dr. Walker was familiar with the mental health system there. By the time the program ended, contact with a mental health center was made, arrangements for the young caller to be seen immediately were completed, and the therapist who would be seeing this young woman was apprised of the situation. The miracle of television.

The audience left the studio quietly while those of us who had been on the program breathed a sigh of relief—but I believe it was a comfortable sigh.

I turned to Michele. She looked at me and smiled. "It wasn't as bad as I thought it might be." Nancy Berchtold came over immediately and put her arms around Michele. Nancy had spoken from the audience. A few years earlier she and her baby had been spared when she was involuntarily hospitalized. She looked tenderly at Michele. "I know this was a difficult thing to do, but I think we reached a lot of people and I just want to say thanks."

Michele said, "I didn't know about your organization. What's it called?"

"Depression After Delivery. 'DAD.'"

"Is there anything I can do to help you?"

"Well, you already have by just being here."

Gradually the group drifted out of the studio and into the hallway adorned with pictures from previous shows. Phil Donahue, who had disappeared briefly as the show ended, returned. Jacket off, red suspenders blazing, he made his way amongst the group thanking people for their participation. When he came to Michele and Jeff his demeanor was different. He spoke softly and I couldn't hear what he was saying. He had first taken Jeff's hand and then put his arm around Michele's shoulder. As he spoke to them Michele looked down at the floor. When she raised her head she was smiling and there were tears streaming down her face.

# EPILOGUE

"How is Michele?" someone will ask.

"Fine," I say. "As well as can be expected," I sometimes respond. "How would you be doing?" I sometimes think.

I have no illusions that I completely understand the way in which this mortification that Michele suffered at her own hands transfigured her soul. Even in the best of circumstances can we ever know another person completely? Do we even know ourselves that way?

Possibly there are hours when she isn't consciously aware of Joshua's ghost. Still she lives. For a while she was unable to spend time with her twin sister's son who was born only a few months after Josh. She is better able to face her older sister's daughter, who at this writing is about five. With the children of friends, some of the joy has returned; it is these relationships that display the irony and tragedy of a woman so naturally gifted with the talent for relating to children, so clearly right for motherhood.

Yes, Michele is okay. With most of her fellow workers there came understanding. As her company suffered hard times she remained on the job, preserved by seniority while others were laid off. Finally her time came.

At first the satisfaction of putting some finishing touches on the house and garden was sufficiently stimulating. Eventually, as the layoff continued, the hours of isolation began to weigh heavily. Fortunately, Michele was able to find new work, nonfactory work, which she enjoyed and has taken up permanently—for now.

Michele and I had our last scheduled appointment in the spring of 1990, but we continued to speak often. Life seemed almost routine. I was comfortably rooted in Bennington, and Michele was quietly living day to day, frequently with a sense of melancholy, occasionally happy, occasionally distraught. Then, a surprise. Ronnie and I were presented with an opportunity to move from Vermont to Florida. After months of endless discussion the lure of the ocean prevailed. Michele and Jeff were amongst the first to know of our decision.

We had dinner at the Remingtons during our final week in Vermont. It was one of those perfect July evenings, cloudless sky, comfortably warm, a light breeze, beautiful light. After a wonderful meal the four of us walked the quiet dusty roads that surrounded their home. Apples were abundant in the orchard, and the occasional horses, which belonged to their few neighbors, would lift their heads to watch our progress. As the Berkshires were turning orange with the sunset, we spoke of friendship, and of our mutual commitment to stay in touch. At one point Michele and I lagged behind and we spoke about this book.

"You know, Michele, we haven't spent much time talking about the book lately, and I sensed that you were uncomfortable."

"I guess there have been times when I haven't wanted to focus on things, and the book makes me do that."

"Maybe we should forget about the book."

She didn't hesitate. She looked at me and said, "Absolutely not. Even though I've wanted to be quiet, and lay off, to see the book published is still something that I want very much. I feel that it's the right thing to do."

I was reminded of Mark Keller's speech to Richard Kelley, and I smiled.

Beyond "How is Michele" there is often a second question. "Will they have more children?" Sometimes the question seems almost whispered. The answer is, probably not. For the first few years Michele and Jeff were afraid—petrified actually—about the prospect of repeating even a haunting refrain of their last experience. With the passage of time, the fracture lines established during their personal earthquake of April 7, 1987, have widened. Michele and Jeff are currently separated.

A few weeks ago I called Michele and told her that the latest version of the book was nearing completion. "I'm worried," I said, "worried about the impact of our book on your life. If we go ahead, if it is published—what will be stirred up?"

There was a pause, then Michele's voice on the other end of the line was quiet and serious. "Sometimes at the store someone will stop and stare at me—or at least I think they are staring. Recently I found out that the woman who had stopped that day was the mother of one of my coworkers. I had known this young man for more than a year and we were friends. He and I had never spoken about the tragedy. He had never acknowledged that he knew anything. Yet that day, when I prodded to learn why his mother looked that way, he said—'she's still angry.'"

Although I knew I asked anyway, "Angry about what?"

"Angry about the baby."

There was again a pause. "It's time to face things again. I don't want to stir things up and I still haven't remembered—and I hope to God I don't. Maybe the book will be provocative—I don't know—but I still feel we should go forward."

Despite Michele's reassurance, when I sent her the copy of the manuscript I continued to worry.

A few days went by and then, the message from my secretary—
"Call Michele." I picked up the phone and dialed, slightly nervous. My concern was unrelieved when I got their answering
tape. "Call me as soon as you can," I said, and hung up.

It was about ten o'clock that evening when the phone rang.
As soon as I heard Michele's voice, I had my answer. There was
a quality—a lightness that I had not ever heard before. It was as
though we had entered another verse of life's poem. She began
to describe for me the things that had been happening in the
past few days. Yes, she felt comfortable with the manuscript, in
fact she was enthusiastic.

"I want to send you something," she said, "something I've
written. I haven't been able to write now for such a long time—
and then suddenly as I was reading, this all poured out." She
began to read. I listened quietly with a lump in my throat.

Michele's words about me are embarrassing, but I am very
appreciative. And I am thankful that I was given the opportunity
to help.

*It is difficult to share with you how I feel from moment
to moment. Perhaps in acknowledging some very
important people, most of whom stood firmly beside me
during the worst of times, times when my physical well-
being was in peril and my thought process was nothing short
of consumed by self-destruction, my heart will be
revealed.*

*To Jeff—the man who stayed when most would have left.
He had every right to leave me, but his heart told him
otherwise. Our tragedy seemed to be a shroud that covered
us and created a separate world that only the two of us
could inhabit. Over time that shroud has lifted, however,
and we have begun to move in different directions.*

*Although our marriage may not survive, I believe our love will.*

To Dr. Carl Burak—what began as a job, an obligation, became a quest to repair a broken, shattered personality and turned into a unique and cherished friendship. This man, one of two who literally saved my life, helped me find the desire to go on. At a time when I did not want to talk to anybody, this gentle man quietly walked into my shattered existence and picked up the first piece. Words could never express my gratitude for his tremendous compassion and willingness to journey with me through a maze of legal nightmares, media humiliation, and dramatic emotional outbursts. No matter what time of day or night I needed him, he was always there for me. I told him once that I wished I could have a miniature version of him to carry around so that when I felt the need we could talk, because I always felt safe around him. My heart is full of gratitude and I can finally say, thank you, Dr. Burak, for saving my life.

To Dr. Fred Loy—the other man who saved my life. I believe that it was pure luck on my side that this gifted surgeon was on call that night—and he was in tune to the fact that something very wrong was going on, something just wasn't right. He too is a gentle man, filled with compassion and patience. I have a special fondness for him and can finally say to him too, thank you, Dr. Loy, for saving my life.

To mom and dad—wonderful parents who never stopped loving me for a moment. They always understood that I was seriously mentally ill for a brief time. They sacrificed greatly in many ways on my behalf and suffered a great deal because of what was happening to me. I love you.

To Joan—my big sister. With intelligence and love you identified the medical expert who would help convince

*the courts that prison was not the appropriate punishment.
Thank you. Your efforts will never be forgotten.*

*To Robert—a fabulous brother who was so looking forward
to being an uncle for the first time. I took that away from
you yet you cried for me and comforted me. You have always
been there for me and given me hope and strength.*

*To Susan—my twin sister. Through no fault of your own,
because of unfortunate lousy timing, we became
strangers. We have lost so much important time. At a time
when my dreams consisted of enjoying days together with
our baby boys and building our friendship. Then the
unthinkable happened and feelings of overwhelming
jealousy invaded my emotions. Time has allowed me to put
the past behind. Although time does not heal, it merely
covers up, I feel ready to pursue the friendship that I caused
us to lose.*

*To Barbara—my dearest friend. Your life was devastated
by my actions yet you never abandoned me. You
committed yourself to seeing me through and getting me to
face the world again. Our friendship has grown strong
because of your stubbornness and your refusal to let me push
you away.*

*To Jeff's family—who were a vital support system to their
son, but who were also ready to help me in any way and
to sacrifice on my behalf. Thank you.*

*To all the medical personnel at the Southern Vermont
Medical Center and Albany Medical Center—all of those
who so dutifully and professionally did their jobs to save my
baby's life the first and second time. And also to anyone
who took care of me in maternity and in emergency. I deeply
regret any emotional stress that I caused and commend
you for your professionalism.*

*To Norman Blais and Mark Keller—although you*

maintained that your professional roles weren't that complicated, from my perspective the path was very complex and each decision was difficult. While you are very good at what you do, you truly cared about me and guided me through every step with genuine concern. I will think of you always with respect and special fondness.

And finally, to Phil Donahue—a man whom I knew only through television until February 1988, when I met you in person. I want to thank you, Mr. Donahue, for the opportunity to appear on your show—the one right decision I made during a time in my life when it seemed that every turn I took was the wrong one, every decision was the wrong choice. You opened the door and I stepped through it. It was very hard but you helped me with your gentle manner and your compassion. I was able to fade out that audience and focus only on you. You were the only one I saw and that helped me carry myself and relay a message. Your show was the right thing to do, and meeting you one-to-one afterwards was the first time in over a year that I started to feel like a somebody again. From my heart, thank you.

In 1987, my dream of motherhood dissolved in a dark psychotic haze that descended slowly. On a rainy day that seemed most certainly eternal, the life of my baby boy was extinguished forever, my whole self-worth shattered, my personality was shaken apart, and my life was forever altered. I would cause so much heartache and sadness to those who love me, that even now, I cannot find forgiveness for myself.

I can never be the same person I was before that tragic day. I can never undo the chaos and grief I brought to the lives of people who never stopped loving me. I can only *hope that this book will help in some way—that some people will be open-minded, willing to take precautions and to gain the knowledge that is so vital. If, through awareness, one life is saved, I will be grateful.*